DEVELOPER ADVOCACY

ESTABLISHING TRUST, CREATING CONNECTIONS, AND INSPIRING DEVELOPERS TO BUILD BETTER

Chris Riley
Chris Tozzi

Apress®

Developer Advocacy: Establishing Trust, Creating Connections, and Inspiring Developers to Build Better

Chris Riley
Boulder, CO, USA

Chris Tozzi
Troy, NY, USA

ISBN-13 (pbk): 978-1-4842-9596-0
https://doi.org/10.1007/978-1-4842-9597-7

ISBN-13 (electronic): 978-1-4842-9597-7

Managing Director, Apress Media LLC: Welmoed Spahr
Acquisitions Editor: Shiva Ramachandran
Development Editor: James Markham
Coordinating Editor: Jessica Vakili

Distributed to the book trade worldwide by Springer Science+Business Media New York, 233 Spring Street, 6th Floor, New York, NY 10013. Phone 1-800-SPRINGER, fax (201) 348-4505, e-mail orders-ny@springer-sbm.com, or visit www.springeronline.com. Apress Media, LLC is a California LLC and the sole member (owner) is Springer Science + Business Media Finance Inc (SSBM Finance Inc). SSBM Finance Inc is a **Delaware** corporation.

For information on translations, please e-mail booktranslations@springernature.com; for reprint, paperback, or audio rights, please e-mail bookpermissions@springernature.com.

Apress titles may be purchased in bulk for academic, corporate, or promotional use. eBook versions and licenses are also available for most titles. For more information, reference our Print and eBook Bulk Sales web page at http://www.apress.com/bulk-sales.

Paper in this product is recyclable

Contents

About the Authors

Chris Riley is obsessed with bringing modern technologies, culture, and practices to tech-enabled enterprises. As a bad-coder-turned-technology-advocate, Chris understands the challenges and needs of modern engineers, as well as how technology fits into the broader business goals of companies in a demanding high-tech world.

Chris speaks and engages with end users regularly in the areas of SRE, DevOps, App Dev, and developer relations. He is one of the original founders of Fixate IO, a marketing agency focused on developer marketing, and currently Senior Manager in Developer Relations at HubSpot. Chris is a regular speaker; contributor to industry blogs such as ContainerJournal.com, DevOps.com, and Sweetcode.io; and overall technical adviser. He is also the host of the podcasts Developers Eating the World, Dissecting DevOps, and Tech A'Sketch.

Chris Tozzi's career has combined two seemingly disparate passions: tech and history. A long-time Linux geek who earned a Ph.D. in French revolutionary history from Johns Hopkins, Chris lived the dream as a tenured professor for several years until boredom with academia prompted him to expand his horizons. Today, Chris keeps his inner historian happy by teaching at a major research university, where his courses cover technology, culture, and society. Meanwhile, he keeps his geek self happy by contributing articles to a variety of technology media sites. He also works as a marketing consultant and technical content developer with Fixate IO, a developer marketing agency that works with a variety of software companies.

Acknowledgments

Jonathan Mooney said in one of my favorite books – and the first to ever make me cry – "Normal sucks. The closer you get to it, the further away you are."

A central aspect of developer advocacy that you will queue into very quickly is that without the presence of being genuine, empathetic, and transparent, you cannot do anything else. While neurodiversity was the biggest challenge in my childhood, it has been the biggest benefit in my adulthood. It started as a tasting menu of misdiagnosis and resulted eventually in the final understanding that living with ADHD, dyslexia, and ASD is exactly what makes developer advocacy a role seemingly architected just for me. Neurodiversity is the biggest gift nature has given me, and I credit that for my experiences, successes, and, ultimately, what I have been able to contribute to this book and other courses and content which preceded it.

But, of course, it has had its challenges. My family has always accepted me for who I am, and my kids have given me a window into the past that has fostered valuable inner-child work, motivation, and positivity: Ava, with her glowing positivity and empathy; Maisie, who analyzes the world in all the unexpected ways no one else could; and Arlo, who, while still very young, has expressed positivity and humor that makes me feel like I am floating and gives me a chance to take myself and life a little less seriously. It was my wife Lauren who gave me these three tiny oracles and put herself in the challenging situation of having a neurodiverse partner. She gave me the space to grow my career, nurtured my soul and body, and challenged me to navigate the intersection between a neurodiverse and a neurotypical society.

Professionally it took a village of individuals to help me take the very rough edges of talent and polish them. In the world of developer relations, the supportive and engaged individuals Andi Mann, Josh Atwell, SJ Morris, Sara Rosso, and Christian Buckley, along with all of the team at Fixate IO and its customers, helped me build a strategy around a very new industry. In the world of business and marketing, where the list is very long, I want to highlight the impact on my career of Don McMahan, Debi Davis, Karen Ng, Joe Budelli, Doug Merit, Alan Shimel, and many more. I owe gratitude, too, to very close friends I let into my inner world, including Chris Tozzi, the annoying but persistent Patrick O'Fallon, April Osmanof, and my podcast and doodle buddy Ashton Rodenhiser.

And finally, I never met either of you, but Steve Jobs and Richard Feynman were my indirect professors in philosophy, business, and innovation.

This may be a nonfiction business book, but the experiences, failures, and nuanced discoveries that it took to bring it together were the collection of many years, a lot of stress, a lot of fun, and bold new industry strategies. Thank you for learning with us, and remember that bringing your full self every day is the foundation of all developer relations and developer advocacy programs; you cannot fake it; sometimes it is messy, but normal sucks.

I welcome you to find me and reach out on LinkedIn, Twitter, my podcast Tech A'Sketch, and a Google search away from my other neurodiversity, DevOps, and DevRel content and courses.

—Chris Riley

If neurodiversity played a crucial role in Chris Riley's ability to succeed in the world of developer advocacy, I've only been able to explore it because many people have given me the opportunity to pursue intellectually diverse pursuits. Ten years ago, I had just received a Ph.D. in French history and planned to spend the rest of my life teaching courses about Napoleon. I still get to do that, but this book is a testament to the many other pursuits I have enjoyed, all of them made possible by folks who generously opened new doors and encouraged me to think in new ways.

A number of people in the tech media industry, especially Charlene O'Hanlon, Sue Troy, Rick Dagley, and Fred Churchville, gave me opportunities to reach broad audiences through writing about technology. Fixate IO allowed me to connect with a variety of tech vendors, who broadened my exposure to different perspectives and ideas. IDC did the same, while putting me in the enviable position of getting paid to share my opinions about software development, cybersecurity, DevOps, and other timely topics. Meanwhile, RPI has allowed me to remain active in teaching a truly diverse array of courses, with lessons spanning Charles I to ChatGPT.

Chris Riley has been the most important enabler and mentor of all. His entrepreneurial spirit launched this project and many of the other most impactful professional ventures of my life.

My wife and children have been patient through it all, even when it wasn't clear that I had a real plan for paying the bills if I veered too far from the cut-and-dry teaching career I had trained for. To them I owe the greatest gratitude.

—Chris Tozzi

What is Developer Advocacy?

It may sound cliché to say that we live in an interconnected world. From the perspective of software development, however, it's worth noting just how remarkably interconnected – and interdependent – software has become over the past decade.

One way of measuring that interconnectedness is to think in terms of how many Application Programming Interfaces, or APIs, developers have access to today. Whereas there were only about 2700 commercially available, public APIs in use in 2011, there are now at least 24,000 APIs. APIs allow programmers to integrate two or more applications, so growth in the proliferation of APIs is a reflection of growing application interdependence.

Meanwhile, trends like widespread use of open source software, which 90 percent of companies now leverage either in wholesale form or as a component in their own, custom software, also reflect the way in which businesses have come to depend on external software development communities. Although noncommercial open source projects don't typically operate developer

© Chris Riley, Chris Tozzi 2023
C. Riley and C. Tozzi, *Developer Advocacy*,
https://doi.org/10.1007/978-1-4842-9597-7_1

advocacy programs, businesses with "open core" models – meaning those that offer commercial products based in part on open source software – are increasingly turning to developer advocates to help strengthen relationships between their open core projects and broader open source communities that might contribute to or engage with those products.

Because trends like these have emerged gradually over the past ten years or so, it can be easy for businesses to overlook them and to fail to appreciate the extent to which companies must now engage with third-party developers to drive business success. But that would be a mistake, because no matter how good your company's in-house developers and software products may be, it's increasingly difficult to thrive today without support and engagement from external developer communities.

Developer Advocacy for the Interconnected Age

That's why developer advocacy has emerged as an increasingly crucial function for businesses of all types. In a world of deeply interconnected and intertwined software ecosystems, developer advocates play a central role in ensuring that companies can interface successfully with the developer communities they depend on.

But because developer advocacy remains a relatively new concept for most businesses and has become vital due to recent trends like widespread use of APIs, it's a function that is easy to miss when planning and structuring technical teams. Most companies know that they need software developers, IT engineers, quality control teams, and so on. But they may not even realize what developer advocacy is, let alone how much developer advocates can do to advance the success of their companies or how to go about creating a developer advocacy function within their organizations.

That's precisely why we wrote this book. Unlike better-established types of roles, developer advocacy does not benefit from an extensive literature explaining how the function works or how to go about implementing it. On the contrary, the very term "developer advocacy" remains foreign to many business executives and IT leaders. We hope through this book to make the term not only into a familiar concept but also into an actionable paradigm that helps companies engage more effectively with developer communities.

What is Developer Advocacy?

We'll explain why we feel qualified to produce this book, and how we accidentally stumbled into the field of developer advocacy, in a moment. First, though, let's define concretely what developer advocacy means and what developer advocates do.

Put simply, developer advocacy is a structured approach to engaging with communities of software developers. Its purpose is to encourage, educate, and support developers who are interested in working with the software that a business produces, requires, or both.

> *Developer Advocacy lets your customers and prospects know that they are not on their own in their adoption journey. Developer advocates are seen as respected peers who are driven to making each customer successful.*

—Josh Atwell, Senior Director, Developer Relations at Equinix

Although developer advocates are typically employed by a business with the goal of enhancing its relationship with developer communities, developer advocates are so called because their job ultimately boils down to becoming advocates for the developers with whom the business wants to engage. This means that in order to do their job well, developer advocates should think not in terms of what their employers want to get developers to do, but rather what developers want and need and how their business's software initiatives can be aligned to meet developers' visions and priorities. In other words, developer advocates should be advocates for developers before the business they serve, rather than advocating for the business to developers.

Developer Advocacy: Past and Present

Although developer advocacy remains a comparatively new type of role, the concepts at its core are not. In certain key respects, the role of developer advocates can be traced back to the 1980s, which is when the field of developer relations emerged under the leadership of figures like Guy Kawasaki. Kawasaki, who was then working at Apple as a tech evangelist, realized that software companies like Apple could be successful only if they engaged systematically with the developer communities on whom they relied to drive the adoption and extension of their platforms. He pioneered the practice of developer relations, or DevRel, as a way to use marketing, community engagement, and partner ecosystems to help external developers work more easily with a company's product.

when people believe in your product, they will help you succeed through credible, continuous, and cost-effective proselytization.

—Guy Kawasaki, *The Art of the Start 2.0: The Time-Tested, Battle-Hardened Guide for Anyone Starting Anything*

In some cases, developer advocacy may be considered synonymous with DevRel, which has been a mainstream function within many software companies for at least the past decade. However, there are key differences between DevRel and developer advocacy in its purest form. One is that developer advocates are expected to be deeply technical; in most cases, they come themselves from a software engineering or IT operations background. In contrast, DevRel is a function that tends to be less technical; DevRel teams tend to rely on marketing skills at least as extensively as they do on technical expertise with software products, platforms, and paradigms.

A second vital difference between DevRel and developer advocacy is that the latter has a strong external focus. The main goal of developer advocates is to think in terms of what developers who are external to a company need and then find out how to serve them. DevRel is different in that DevRel practitioners tend to think more often about what the business's own goals are and then try to convince external developers to embrace them. This difference in focus may seem small, but it breeds a fundamentally different mindset between developer relations teams and developer advocates.

Developer Advocacy As a Unique Function

Because developer advocacy diverges from DevRel in terms of skill sets, focus, goals, and approach, it's a mistake in most cases to lump developer advocacy into DevRel – or, worse, to assume that because your business has DevRel, it's necessarily performing developer advocacy too.

Instead, developer advocacy should be treated as a distinct function within the business. It should be as structured, scalable, and repeatable as peer functions, like software engineering, sales, and marketing.

Unfortunately, this is not often how businesses approach developer advocacy. The lack of awareness and experience surrounding the role, combined with a perception among some leaders that developer advocates are hard-to-find "superstars" who possess the unique talents required to engage with developer communities, has caused some organizations to avoid treating developer advocacy as a standard function. The fact that it can be difficult to quantify the impact of developer advocacy is yet another reason why some businesses shy away from treating it as a distinct role or function.

But to consign developer advocates to vaguely defined roles, and to fail to integrate them systematically into the broader business, is a mistake. It's only by dedicating a function to advocates that businesses can reliably hire and support them. Treating advocacy as a function is also important for helping to scale the number of developer advocates a business has in hand – a critical consideration given that hiring a single developer advocate is often not enough.

In addition, when developer advocacy is structured as a stand-alone function, it becomes easier for businesses to appreciate the value of the role, even when advocates fail to perform magic (as most do, because engaging developer communities requires sustained, continuous initiatives that don't often yield watershed changes in the way developers approach a software platform). Developer advocacy is similar to functions like product marketing or public and analyst relations, whose impact is also difficult to quantify, but which organizations nonetheless recognize as important functions because they perform work that influences the direction of the business in a "long-tail" fashion. When developer advocates are allowed to function similarly to these other types of roles, the contributions of advocates to the business become easier for leaders to recognize and appreciate.

Who Needs Developer Advocates?

It may be tempting to assume that the only companies that can benefit from developer advocates are large software businesses that sell large, complex platforms – companies like Apple, Google, or Microsoft. In reality, however, any company that sells to or otherwise engages with technical audiences can benefit from a developer advocacy role. If your business offers APIs that third-party developers can use to integrate with your products or services, you can benefit from advocacy. Or even if you don't offer specific platform integration channels, but third-party developers play a role in helping to implement, support, or customize your product, developer advocacy can help you to engage with those developers more effectively. Businesses that offer open source products, or that depend on open source communities to build tools or products that they use or support, also stand much to gain from developer advocacy.

Without a developer advocacy function, businesses may struggle to build confidence in their product within technical communities. Third-party developers or engineers may wonder whether a business truly believes in its own product and wants to see others create extensions or integrations with it. They may also be unsure how to go about working with a platform, or where to direct questions if they can't find the information they need in documentation. And they may struggle to determine which integration possibilities even exist, without technical experts like developer advocates to guide and inspire them.

In contrast, when well implemented, the developer advocacy function ensures that businesses meet developer expectations in a systematic way. Advocacy supports software platform growth and maximizes the quality of relationships by, first, helping businesses to understand where external developer audiences exist and then providing content and channels to make those audiences aware of the business's platform. From there, advocates can help to inspire external users and provide them with a sense of "the art of the possible" in regard to building on top of a software platform. They help developers feel excited about what they can create. And once creation is underway – once developers are already engaged members of a business's software ecosystem – advocates sustain smooth, ongoing relationships by identifying further integration opportunities, playing a hand in support, and ensuring that developers' feedback informs future platform architecture changes or feature updates.

In pursuing these goals, the developer advocacy function benefits a number of other functions across the business. It provides sales teams with subject matter experts who don't need to meet sales quotas and therefore stand nothing from telling the truth about a company's product or platform. In this respect, advocates can help sales teams better understand the products they sell from the perspective of their customers – even if internal company messaging about the products is different from the way customers perceive them. Likewise, advocates can help sales teams to understand complex technical concepts and explain them effectively to prospects.

In a similar fashion, developer advocacy helps marketers to develop more effective messaging. Advocates can serve as sounding boards for marketing teams who are working on campaigns or marketing content, helping to ensure that marketing initiatives actually speak to the developers they intend to reach. At the same time, advocates can amplify marketing messaging and serve as vectors for sharing content. In many cases, they also develop technical marketing content themselves, addressing a need that marketers often cannot meet because they do not come from a technical background.

For product support teams, developer advocates play the absolutely crucial role of helping to address questions that arise from customers but that support teams aren't always ready to answer because they involve undocumented features or unexpected problems. Because developer advocates use products themselves, and because they understand the language of developers in a unique way, they can help to troubleshoot vexing support issues, as well as guide support teams in finding the most effective ways of engaging developers. That said, it's important to avoid the mistake of treating developer advocates merely as a type of "elite" support staff, because support is only one of the many functions that advocates can help to enhance.

Product teams, too, can work more effectively with the help of developer advocates. The goal of product teams is to identify what customers want and then build products and features to meet those demands. To that end, product managers often collect feedback from customers. However, because they don't engage day in and day out with customers, their ability to understand the perspectives of their users tends to be limited. In addition, product teams have a tendency to be biased toward their own products, and they may sometimes assume that if users aren't getting what they want out of a product, it's because they aren't using the product in the way its designers intended, not because there is a problem with the product itself. From this perspective, developer advocates help to keep product teams honest and guide them in seeing their products through the eyes of their users. They can also provide more substantive external feedback about products than product management teams can obtain through rudimentary feedback processes like surveys or one-off customer interviews.

Finally, engineering teams, whose job is to build the platforms that developer advocates seek to promote, can work more effectively and efficiently with the help of developer advocates. As with product management teams, advocates can help engineering teams to see better how users perceive their platforms. Because developers are on the front line – and because they have deep technical expertise equivalent to that of engineers – advocates are deeply aware of the bugs, challenges, and missing features that impact how third-party developers engage with a product.

Common Mistakes in Developer Advocacy

Deciding to implement developer advocacy as a function within your business is not enough to support other teams in the way described previously, or to guarantee successful engagement with developer communities. To achieve those goals, it's critical to avoid common pitfalls associated with creating and running developer advocacy programs. We'll discuss these mistakes in greater detail throughout the book, but we'd like to foreground them now in order to provide further context on what developer advocacy looks like and why it should be treated as a unique function.

One common mistake surrounding developer advocacy is to treat developer advocates solely as members of the technical part of a business, as opposed to experts who can support both technical and nontechnical functions. As we explained earlier, although advocates are themselves technical, they play pivotal roles in helping to support teams like sales and marketing, too. If you don't ensure that advocates engage with your entire business, you limit the value that they deliver.

Equally problematic is abandoning the developer advocacy function shortly after implementing it. Because developer advocates don't typically deliver easily quantifiable benefits, and because it can take many months or even years for advocates to demonstrate their value, business leaders may fail to sustain their investment in advocacy long enough to realize its full benefit. The result is a false start from which it is very difficult to recover, because restarting the developer advocacy function after a failed initial attempt is very difficult. It's hard to hire new advocates if they know that your company previously pulled the plug on its advocacy program. It's also challenging to get renewed buy-in for advocacy from within the business if the initial program failed.

A third challenge that developer advocacy programs often encounter is an inability to scale. It's common to start off with just one developer advocate. But more – perhaps dozens – may be necessary for businesses that depend extensively on third-party developer engagement and that need to be able to meet and support external developers through a variety of channels and programs.

Likewise, as we noted previously, it's a mistake to reduce the developer advocate role to one of product support. Although developer advocates can, and should, help to troubleshoot complex support issues that the support team can't resolve on its own, advocates shouldn't be treated as mere extensions of the support team. Thus, businesses should expect advocates to serve as champions of external developers when they run into major technical problems, but not to be the go-to support staff that developers approach for routine issues.

It's also problematic to treat developer advocates as extension of the marketing team. Although advocates do play a role in helping to promote products, they are not marketers, and if developers perceive them as such, the developer advocacy function could backfire. Indeed, part of the value of employing developer advocates in the first place is that developers are often "allergic" to engagement that comes off as generic marketing. They want to engage with businesses through genuine connections rooted in technical content, as opposed to ads, blog posts, or conference presentations that sing the praises of a business's software in a nakedly promotional way. So, while developer advocates can help marketing teams to understand how to engage more effectively with developer audiences, businesses should avoid deploying technical advocates in the same way that they use marketing teams, or expecting advocates to parrot the language of marketers.

Measuring the Business Impact of Developer Advocates

We said earlier that it's usually difficult to quantify the impact of developer advocacy in a simple way. That's true, but it doesn't mean that businesses can't measure developer advocacy success. On the contrary, there are several practical ways to track the impact of developer advocates on your business.

One is to measure activity related to your API or other integration channels. By tracking how many external developers are using your platform, as well as which specific features they are engaging with, you can assess whether the types of engagement that your advocates are pursuing are effective. For example, if you've recently rolled out a new integration feature and you've relied primarily on developer advocates to introduce that feature to your developer community, it's relatively easy to determine how effectively the advocates have achieved that goal by tracking how often developers use the new feature.

Along similar lines, you can track the breadth of solutions that external developers build using your platform. Advocates inspire developers to build better solutions by designing and delivering best practices. They also inspire developers to consider new solutions. When developers create new types of features or integrations, instead of simply building new implementations of integrations that already exist, you know that developer advocates are doing their job well.

A third key measure of developer advocacy success is churn rates, meaning how often developers abandon your platform. Given that the central purpose of developer advocates is to build trust with developers and ensure that they are represented and heard by other stakeholders within your company, lower churn rates reflect developer advocacy success. When developers remain committed to your platform over the long term, it's a sign that your developer advocates are effectively guiding developers in envisioning new solutions to build, helping them to work through challenges effectively, encouraging them to adopt new integrations that you introduce, and instilling confidence in your business as a vendor that will be around to support its developer community over the long term.

Finally, businesses can evaluate advocates' impact by assessing how integrations with their products are implemented. APIs are complex by nature, and they tend to grow more complex over time. Documentation may provide external developers with basic guidance on how to use APIs, but it's often not enough to ensure consistent integration techniques that align with best practices.

Effective developer advocates fill this gap by creating resources that do help to guide developer audiences as they use your business's APIs and other integration channels. They help to elevate best practices, and they can help customers from an architectural perspective in understanding how to build their applications so that they are high quality and achieve high performance through your APIs. Thus, the more often you encounter integrations that deviate from best practices, or that fail to meet the expectations of their developers, the lower the effectiveness of your developer advocacy.

There is no substitute for a well-focused developer advocacy team to build a delightful user experience throughout the customer adoption journey. Advocates let customers know that they are a priority and their needs are being met – even when challenges may exist in your product(s). This is critical to building trust with your customers and motivating them to become advocates for your products and company.

—Josh Atwell, Senior Director, Developer Relations at Equinix

Why This Book?

As we noted, resources dedicated to helping businesses implement and sustain developer advocacy programs are far and few between. Filling the need for information on this topic was our primary motivation in creating this book. We want to help businesses engage with developers more effectively.

Why? Because a world where businesses are good at getting external developers to integrate with their platforms is a world with better integrations and a more positive experience from users' perspectives. The clear trend is toward ever-more interconnectedness and interdependencies between software platforms – not to mention ever-more-complex APIs, which make building effective integrations even more difficult in the absence of effective guidance. Without a function dedicated to helping developers make the best use of integrations, we'll end up with buggier software, integrations that fail to take full advantage of all of the platform features available, and slow rates and innovation, among other issues that lead to a lower-quality user experience. Developer advocacy, however, ensures the opposite – better integrations, better performance, and better user experience.

Admittedly, we don't have a particular reason to care whether *your* company engages effectively with developers. We probably don't work for you, and to be frank, we could put our time to more profitable use by developing advocacy content – which is what we specialize in – rather than writing the book you're reading. But, again, we do care deeply about ensuring that integrations drive positive user experiences – because we are, like everyone else, software users who want a good experience – and we see developer advocacy as an essential resource for businesses that want developers to create excellent integrations based on their platforms.

Between the two of us, the authors of this text have three decades of experience in selling and marketing to technical audiences. We hail from technical backgrounds ourselves, but we've spent the bulk of our careers helping developers learn about and engage with technology, rather than building technology.

Over the course of that experience, we've noticed the many inconsistencies surrounding developer marketing, advocacy, and relations. We've worked with companies that attempt, with little success, to make developer advocacy a function of marketing teams that lack the technical depth necessary to speak developers' language and that fail to understand the unique needs of developers as an audience.

Likewise, we've been a part of organizations that have attempted to force their engineers to moonlight as evangelists for their platforms within technical communities. We've found in that case that most engineers lack a real desire to perform advocacy work on top of their technical jobs. They also typically do not have the nontechnical skills necessary to excel in developing content and programs that engage developers.

And we have done our fair share of work in the developer relations field, too – which, as we've said, is too often taken as a synonym for or alternative to developer advocacy. But the reality is that developer advocacy requires a different approach, with a different set of goals, from developer relations. That's why it deserves its own book.

We've organized this book into three major parts: understanding, starting and scaling. The first part (which constitutes the chapter you're reading, along with Chapter 2) aims to provide an understanding of what developer advocacy is and why it's important. The second part (Chapters 3–6) covers various aspects of getting started with developer advocacy, such as how to structure a developer advocacy team and how to create interfaces between developer advocates and other functions within the business. The final part (Chapters 7–10) explains how to scale developer advocate programs to maximize their potential, as well as how to measure their success.

So, no matter which point you're currently at on the developer advocacy journey – whether you've already implemented a developer advocate function or (as is more likely) you're exploring the possibility and wondering how to go about it – this book is for you. Drawing from our experiences in the industry, as well as our analysis of what other businesses have gotten right (and wrong) in the realm of developer advocacy, this book provides actionable guidance that business and technology leaders can use to understand the benefits of advocacy, identify what goes into the function, and learn how to maximize the success of developer advocate teams.

Becoming a Developer Advocate

Even by the standards of the IT industry, where unorthodox career paths are not uncommon, the approaches that individuals may take to become developer advocates are many and varied. There is no specific college degree that developer advocates need to earn, nor are there – at least as of yet – training or certificate programs dedicated to developed advocacy.

What this means is that many people can potentially become developer advocates, regardless of their career status or educational history. Unlike roles such as software engineering or marketing, developer advocacy careers aren't shaped by rigid formulas.

That said, developer advocates should have particular qualities, such as strong communication skills and a passion for education. Technical expertise is also critical – and for that reason, most developer advocates worked previously as engineers – although the specific skills required vary depending on which developer communities advocates engage with.

© Chris Riley, Chris Tozzi 2023
C. Riley and C. Tozzi, *Developer Advocacy*,
https://doi.org/10.1007/978-1-4842-9597-7_2

This chapter explains what it takes to become a developer advocate. Although there is no specific set of boxes to check or a recipe to follow to pursue a career in advocacy, there are particular considerations to weigh and strategies to pursue. We explain them in the following by discussing the key attributes of a developer advocate, as well as how advocates and aspiring advocates can cultivate particular interests and talents in order to enter the field of advocacy.

Although much of the material in this chapter is tailored toward individuals considering work as developer advocates, this chapter is not just for advocates themselves. It's also for business stakeholders, who need to understand what advocates do, and which qualities they bring to the table, in order to plan and execute effective developer advocacy initiatives.

Attributes of a Developer Advocate

A good developer advocate is motivated by empathy. They understand the challenges that their audience face and work to make it easier to solve those challenges. An advocate does this because they truly want their customers to both feel, and be, successful.

—Josh Atwell, Senior Director, Developer Relations at Equinix

Although in many ways developer advocates occupy a unique role within modern organizations, in another sense, they represent a combination of three existing functions – but they execute on these functions in unique ways that make developer advocates different from other people working within these roles:

- **Marketing:** To a certain extent, developer advocates are marketers. However, because developer audiences are typically "allergic" to material that looks or feels like marketing fluff, a key skill of advocates must be the ability to communicate a software vendor's messaging and brand value to developer communities without sounding like a traditional marketer. The best way to do this is to focus on technical topics and highlight how the vendor's platform stands out in a genuinely technical sense – while also recognizing its technical shortcomings. The capacity to engage authentically with developers on a technical level is the key factor that makes developer advocates different from conventional marketers.

- **Sales:** Although developer advocates aren't salespeople and don't typically play a formal role in the sales process, they may help to generate leads by encouraging interest in a vendor's platform among external users who eventually become customers. In addition, because advocates are able to explain and demonstrate the technical complexities of platforms in ways that traditional sales teams often cannot, advocates may be asked to play a role in nurturing leads or closing sales, especially in cases where businesses sell to technical decision-makers.

- **Support:** As Chapter 1 noted, it's a mistake to treat developer advocates as support staff. Support should be the realm of separate team members. Nonetheless, advocates can provide guidance for support teams with regard to identifying the most serious issues users are experiencing and helping support staff to resolve them.

At a high level, then, developer advocates must think and act partly as marketers, partly as salespeople, and partly as customer or end-user support specialists. And unsurprisingly, many individuals who pursue developer advocacy roles come from backgrounds in marketing, sales, or support.

But that doesn't mean that anyone with experience in the areas described previously is a good candidate to work in developer advocacy. To excel in developer advocate roles, candidates should also possess the following key attributes – some of which come naturally and others of which can be actively cultivated.

Technical Knowledge

First and foremost, it's critical for developer advocates to possess technical expertise specific to the platform or products that they evangelize to developer communities. Without deep technical knowledge, it's impossible to engage with developers in a way that feels genuine and authentic to them. Individuals who are passionate about a platform but who don't understand its inner workings in a technical sense would function better in traditional marketing or sales positions than developer advocacy.

Importantly, the essentiality of technical skills for advocacy doesn't mean that advocates need to have worked in a deeply technical role like software engineering prior to pursuing advocacy work. Some advocates were former developers or engineers, but others come from product management, product marketing, or sales engineering backgrounds wherein they mastered key technical concepts related to the platform that they promote.

The importance of technical skills should also not be interpreted to mean that developer advocates necessarily have to be qualified to help build the platform they advocate for. It just means that they must understand how it works in a technical sense.

To put this in context, consider an advocate employed by a business that sells a cloud storage platform. To advocate effectively for the platform to third-party developers, it's important that the advocate understand technical concepts like the kind of cloud storage (object, file, database, and so on) that the platform supports, which kinds of APIs the platform offers to third-party developers, and which security controls it supports for controlling access to data. This expertise is necessary for explaining the platform to technical audiences and discussing how they can use it.

However, the advocate doesn't necessarily need to know how to write API calls for the platform or how to develop new native features for it. That level of depth – which would typically only be possessed by the platform's own internal developers – is not essential for engaging with external developers who might want to use the platform in some way.

Developer Awareness

Advocates don't necessarily need to come from a software development background, but they do need a basic understanding of how software development works, at least in an organizational sense. Even if advocates don't have experience actually managing software projects, an understanding of how projects operate is critical for understanding what third-party developers want and need and how the platform they are advocating for fits into software development projects.

Thus, advocates need to know how teams of developers are organized and how they manage development operations. They should understand what terms like "sprint" or "release cycle" mean. They should master the concept of continuous delivery and how modern organizations use it. And they should have an understanding of how software releases are tested and validated prior to deployment.

Passion for Communication

Stereotypically, people with technical skills are introverted. They like to work in isolation, and they are not experts in communication.

Good developer advocates don't fit this stereotype. Although they must possess technical chops, they should also be passionate about engaging with others, and they should have a knack for doing so in a friendly, charismatic way. The ability to communicate effectively in multiple mediums – online, via in-person presentations, through information conversation, and more – is also vital.

These traits tend to come naturally to individuals who enjoy helping others to solve problems and learn. If you're searching for a developer advocate – or you're wondering whether you might have a future in developer advocacy – think about questions like how effectively the prospective advocate answers technical questions in online forums, or how passionate they are about explaining technical concepts without being formally tasked with doing so. People who are organically inclined to share technical knowledge, and who are drawn to opportunities to do so in both online and in-person contexts, are great fits for developer advocacy.

Creativity

Developer advocates must be creative. They must be able to think innovatively and independently about questions like which paths of engagement are most effective for reaching outside audiences and which communication strategies work best for audiences with varying levels of prior experience using a product or platform.

Creativity is an especially important attribute for advocates given that there is no standard formula for advocates to follow and that the advocacy function remains so new at many businesses. Advocates must chart and execute their own strategies, and they must adapt those strategies to the particular businesses and platforms they support. Outside-the-box thinking is crucial in this regard.

Empathy

Not all third-party developers react positively to engagement by developer advocates. Some may actively resist or resent advocacy initiatives because they view them as marketing in disguise. In other cases, developer advocates may find themselves tasked with responding to or engaging with external developers who have not had a positive experience using a platform.

In situations like these, empathy – meaning the ability to see things through the lenses of others and understand their perspective – becomes an essential attribute. Developer advocates who are empathetic are positioned to respond to negativity or criticism without becoming defensive – which is almost never a winning strategy, because it usually causes critics to double-down on their attacks against a platform or vendor. Rather than going on the defensive in the face of criticism, advocates should be primed to employ empathy as a means of genuinely appreciating critical viewpoints and responding to them in a way that makes all third-party developers – no matter how they view the platform – feel respected and supported.

Peer-Centric Mindset

The best developer advocates think of themselves as the peers of the developers they advocate to. In other words, advocates view themselves as seeking the same things – specifically, education and guidance about how to use a software platform – as the audiences they engage.

Having a peer-centric mindset is important given that advocates are in a unique role within the communities they support. As an advocate, it can be easy to wander into the position of viewing yourself as smarter or more qualified than third-party developers, since you have an understanding of your business's platform that they lack. But that perspective undercuts the ability of advocates to engage organically and empathically with third-party developers, because it's much harder to see things from the developers' perspective for advocates who don't think of themselves as "one of them."

A peer-focused mindset is also important because it helps to ensure that advocates don't think of themselves as "celebrities" or influencers within technical communities. Good advocates may eventually gain a status that gives them influence over how developers think and what they prioritize, but advocates should not start from the position that their main mission is to gain prominence as thought leaders within the communities they engage. Instead, they should focus on giving third-party developers the information they need to learn about and use a platform and then let influence and thought leadership grow organically from there.

Humbleness and Humility

Empathy and a peer-centric mindset go hand in hand with a humble attitude, which is another core attribute of developer advocates. While there is nothing wrong with celebrating one's work and feeling a sense of importance as an advocate – indeed, advocates should do these things in order to maximize their impact – advocates should not be inclined to view themselves as heroes or to overstate their accomplishments.

Instead, advocates should think of themselves as contributors toward a collective goal that is about much more than themselves: helping broad communities of third-party developers use a platform. When advocates behave with humbleness and humility, it's much easier for developers to view them as an authentic source of guidance and support, rather than as people out to promote themselves above all else.

Transitioning into Advocacy

How does someone who possesses the core attributes of a developer advocate actually become a developer advocate?

Again, there's no simple or fixed answer. You can't simply earn a certain credential to enter into developer advocacy. Plus, given that many developer advocates begin in other roles and are promoted internally rather than being hired into developer advocacy through public job postings, the path to a developer advocate job is not as consistent or straightforward as for many other types of roles.

But aspiring advocates can engage in specific activities and practices that are key for transitioning into advocacy roles. In the following, we outline three broad contexts – personal lives, professional settings, and social settings – where prospective advocates can hone their skills.

Personal Advocacy Skills

In personal life, the key focus of aspiring advocates should be on developing the attributes described previously.

In particular, prospective advocates should practice developing humility, authenticity, and empathy. Although these attributes may come more easily to some individuals than others, they can all be learned or cultivated to a certain extent.

Humility, for example, can be practiced by learning to accept compliments with gratitude and poise while avoiding overt self-celebration or promotion. If you can leverage personal successes as opportunities to operate with humility, you're also likely to excel in a developer advocacy role where humility is an important attribute.

Likewise, empathy can be learned by striving to see affairs through the perspective of others. In personal settings, developers should practice the art of assuming that people who disagree with them are not wrong but are simply of a different opinion.

As for authenticity, learning to say what you mean – and backing up what you say with action – is a great way to develop your ability to operate as an authentic person. When you carry an air of authenticity in your personal life, you can bring the same aura to work as a developer advocate.

In addition to cultivating these personality traits, aspiring advocates should invest time in self-education. As a developer advocate, you'll need to master new concepts and keep pace with continuously changing technology. The greater your ability to self-teach, the more effective you'll be at advocacy work.

Professional Practices

No matter which role you work in currently, there are concrete actions you can take in a professional capacity to prime yourself for a role in advocacy.

The most important initiative to undertake is learning to work as part of a team. Although many businesses employ just a single developer advocate, advocates must constantly interface with other stakeholders within the business (like marketing and support teams), as well as with third-party developers. To prepare for this work, aspiring advocates need experience working as part of a broader organization.

It's possible that you're already accustomed to working as part of a team. But if you're not, seize opportunities to work closely with others in professional settings by, for example, volunteering to join projects that involve multiple stakeholders or serving as the liaison between your business unit and others.

A second vital practice that prospective advocates should engage in at work is creating technical content, such as blogs and videos. In some cases, this type of work turns individuals into developer advocates before they even realize it, because writing blogs and other content about a company's platform or products is a means of communicating and engaging with external developer communities.

This doesn't mean that you have to start creating content aimed specifically at third-party developers to set yourself on the path to a developer advocacy role. Experience creating any type of technically oriented content – including material that is shared only inside your business, rather than with external audiences – qualifies you for potential advocacy work.

Finally, aspiring advocates should look for opportunities to engage in product marketing. Although advocates aren't product marketers, many aspects of their work align with product marketing. And unlike other elements of advocacy work – such as understanding technical concepts – product marketing is a unique function that can be difficult to understand without firsthand experience. Wherever possible, then, prospective advocates should seek ways to work alongside product marketers in their organization and understand how they work to shape the business's platform.

Social

If personal and professional settings create opportunities for learning or sharpening the key skills of advocates, social settings – which include in-person social events like conferences as well as virtual social networks – are where aspiring advocates can most easily show off their attributes and bring them to bear on the real world.

Leveraging social contexts to this end starts with establishing a social presence online. This book focuses on using LinkedIn for this purpose, but there are of course other platforms or sites where aspiring advocates should operate actively. In some cases, specific platforms may be particularly important; for example, advocates interested in open source software will need a presence on GitHub, which most open source projects use to manage their code.

Likewise, to the extent feasible, aspiring advocates should seek to establish a presence in real-world social contexts. They should attend industry events relevant to the technologies or communities that interest them. Events that bring together a global audience are ideal, but even local events, like meetup groups, can be a place to start for advocates who want to make themselves known as members of a particular community.

Establishing a social presence online and in real life is just the first step toward setting yourself up for work as a developer advocate. Equally important is cultivating a point of view about the technology or platform you wish to promote and then weaving that viewpoint into the conversations and content you engage in or produce. For example, you might have strong views about making software accessible or optimizing application quality. By focusing on a specific viewpoint that matters to technical audiences, you begin to establish yourself as someone who has relevant knowledge to share within technical communities.

Demonstrating your engagement with others is part of the equation too. Demonstration means having conversations in public and responding to engagement with content you produce. As an aspiring advocate, you want to make yourself known as an individual who actively, empathetically, and authentically participates in technical conversations, not someone who merely produces technical content.

You should also, of course, strive to engage with a broad audience. You don't want to have conversations online with a select group of people.

That said, you don't need a large number of followers or "influencer-level" status to succeed on the road to advocacy. What matters much more than follower count is the ability to have genuine conversations about topics that interest a technical audience. Whether the audience you reach consists of ten people or ten thousand isn't important, especially for someone working to become an advocate. What is important is showing that you know how to speak to technical audiences.

Once you've established a social presence and point of view, look for opportunities to stand out in special ways within the technical conversations that take place online and in-person. For instance, you might seek out opportunities to be a guest on a podcast relevant to a particular technical community by contacting the podcast host. Or contributing code to open source projects can be a way to raise your profile.

As you do all of the aforementioned to establish yourself as someone capable of advocacy work, strive to treat the process as more than a means to an end. In other words, don't build a social presence and establish a point of view just because it will get you noticed within technical communities. Instead, if you really are cut out to be a developer advocate, you will do these things because they organically interest you and you genuinely enjoy them. If you don't, or they feel forced, advocacy may not be a fit for you.

Examples of Becoming an Advocate

To contextualize what it looks like in practice to become a developer advocate, let's look at a few examples of how people in other roles commonly make the transition.

As an Engineer...

If you come from an engineering background, you already have the technical expertise necessary to thrive as an advocate. What you'll likely need to develop, however, is the ability to turn your technical knowledge into content that engages other developers. You'll also probably need to establish a social presence, since most engineers aren't especially active on in-person or virtual social forums.

As a Sales Engineer...

Sales engineers – meaning salespeople with an engineering background who specialize in selling technical products – have both technical skills and a passion for communicating with external stakeholders. In this sense, sales engineers are ideal candidates for developer advocacy roles.

The key challenge they tend to face, however, is learning to share technical knowledge for sharing's own sake, rather than to drive sales. As a sales engineer, then, you'll need to practice creating and sharing technical content that engages audiences intrinsically and that is not tied to generating revenue. You can – and should – have technical opinions, but they should not serve sales goals; they should instead reflect your own, authentic perspective, uncoupled from the sales agenda.

As a Product Marketer...

Product marketers, who specialize in raising awareness about technical products and sharing brand messaging, usually have a great sense of creating compelling content. But the content they build isn't always deeply technical, because the audiences they market to often consist of stakeholders who are not themselves practitioners but are instead in management roles.

To transition to an advocacy role, then, product marketers need to focus on creating content with as much technical depth as possible. They should also, like sales engineers, learn to decouple their content and technical perspectives from a specific business agenda. That's the only way to craft truly authentic content and engage with audiences that are turned off instantly by anything that feels like marketing collateral.

A Personal Story

One of the authors discovered that his career path went in parallel to the growth of advocacy as a role. Advocacy did not exist when I started my career, but over the 15 years marketing to, building for, and selling to software developers, I naturally participated in all the aspects of advocacy. Starting out as a software developer, I was a great architect but a bad coder. What ended up happening is I also had the ability to communicate the technical details and offer the art of the possible quite well. This got me pulled into sales calls. I was also great at troubleshooting; this got me pulled into support. And eventually I was good at messaging; this got me pulled into marketing efforts. And I often had great product feature ideas; this got me pulled into product management. I participated in all these roles by title for a time. Eventually after Guy's book *The Art of the Start*, VCs started pushing the role of tech evangelism on tech companies. It became a common role in startups and then in large tech companies and then evolved into the multidisciplinary function DevRel. I have had my time to shine in the content management, CRM, and DevOps spaces. But now I have backed away from the stage, and my favorite thing to do is to take raw advocacy talent and foster even better advocacies than I ever was.

Conclusion: The Journey to Advocacy

No one becomes a developer advocate overnight, and no one is born with all of the unique traits of a developer advocate.

Instead, becoming a developer advocate is a process that takes time and that requires the cultivation of specific skills and practices. Aspiring advocates must engage in work that establishes them as authentic, empathetic, and humble members of technical communities in order to gain the expertise necessary to advocate for a platform within those communities.

In some cases, advocates stumble into their roles almost by accident because they find themselves sharing technical knowledge and opinions simply because they enjoy it. But not all advocates follow this path. Others come from backgrounds, like engineering, where engagement with external developer communities is typically not a priority and where prospective advocates need to make a point of cultivating the specific attributes and experiences necessary to engage with third-party developers.

The bottom line is that no matter what your background, you have the potential to become a developer advocate, as long as you have a genuine passion for participating in technical conversations. You don't need to fit a specific profile to succeed in the advocacy field.

If you have the drive necessary to become an advocate but are wondering how you actually land a role as an advocate – or if you're a business stakeholder looking to find people with advocacy promise and work with them to build an advocacy function in your organization – read on to the next chapter, which explains how technology companies can find and support developer advocates or aspiring advocates to create advocacy programs.

Starting a Developer Advocacy Program

Even for experienced business leaders, launching a developer advocacy program can be tremendously challenging. Unlike more traditional business functions – such as sales, marketing, and engineering – there is no established "blueprint" to follow for integrating developer advocates into an organization. Even more challenging is the lack of simple metrics for quantifying the impact of developer advocates, which makes it hard in many cases to justify developer advocacy initiatives and to keep them growing over time. Likewise, and for related reasons, scaling from a program that includes just one or a handful of developer advocates to a full-scale advocacy unit is no mean feat.

The good news is that all of these challenges are possible to overcome, so long as businesses plan for them from the start of their developer advocacy journey. Although there is no singular strategy or specific set of steps that all

© Chris Riley, Chris Tozzi 2023
C. Riley and C. Tozzi, *Developer Advocacy*,
https://doi.org/10.1007/978-1-4842-9597-7_3

businesses must follow when starting a developer advocacy program – on the contrary, there are many viable approaches – there are several key principles to bear in mind and actionable practices that encourage the successful launch and growth of developer advocacy as a business function.

This chapter spells out those principles and practices in order to provide a comprehensive overview of what it takes to get started with developer advocacy from the perspective of the business. We discuss how developer advocacy programs typically first emerge within a business and then how they grow over time. We also explain how to structure developer advocacy programs and measure their impact in a way that makes it possible to assess their impact and justify continued investment. And we detail the process that businesses typically follow for interviewing and hiring developer advocates, including salary expectations business leaders should expect to meet for advocates and how to establish promotional paths for developers within the business.

Beginnings: Advocacy Starts As a Team of One

In most cases, advocacy programs are not the result of a deliberate, top-down effort by executives or managers to add a developer advocacy function to their businesses. Instead, advocacy emerges organically starting with the initiative of a single individual, who becomes the business's first developer advocate as part of a business experiment.

These experiments with developer advocacy typically result in part from a desire by the type of person described in the previous chapter – an individual with a background in engineering, sales, and/or marketing who aspires to become an advocate – to engage with third-party developer communities. The experiment with advocacy may also reflect an awareness on the part of businesses that their competitors have advocacy programs and/or that there is an opportunity for the business to enhance its relationship with third-party developers.

Still, because business leaders lack a clear understanding of exactly how developer advocacy will fit within their organizations, and because there is no established script of playbook to follow when launching developer advocacy programs, initial support for and investment in developer advocacy tends to be limited. The advocate's immediate managers may be supportive, but the rest of the business often does not see developer advocacy as a priority, at least in the early stages of an advocacy program.

That said, it's certainly possible for higher-level managers or executives to initiate a developer advocacy program (and indeed, this is becoming more common as more businesses recognize the importance of advocacy). But even when they do, it's likely that they will start small, given the lack of a clear path for starting an advocacy program and integrating advocates into the larger organization, as well as the difficulty of quantifying the value of advocates in a way that other executives and investors in the business can appreciate. So, even in cases where there is a top-down effort to start an advocacy team, the team often involves just one or a small handful of individuals, and the initiative is usually treated at first as an experiment that needs to justify itself in order to turn into a permanent function within the business.

Either way, a one-person developer advocacy team may achieve some success in the short term by achieving greater engagement with third-party developers. But in the long run, small-scale advocacy programs are not a recipe for success. Relying on just a single advocate places the business at risk because its ability to engage with third-party developers depends almost entirely on a single person and their influence. Single-person advocacy teams may appear impressive if the advocate happens to be a "celebrity" within the business's developer community. But if that person leaves the company, or does not maintain the necessary reputation within developer communities to advocate effectively for the business's APIs and products, the organization's developer advocacy program will quickly turn into a failure.

Thus, the key challenge that businesses must conquer in order to launch a successful advocacy program is turning single-person advocacy teams into a larger, more reliable, and more systematic function within the business. In other words, they must forge a bridge that evolves developer advocacy from a small-scale experiment into a permanent business function. That's what the rest of this chapter explains how to do.

Set Actionable Goals

The first step in nurturing a small-scale, experimental developer advocacy program so that it grows into a mature business function is to determine exactly what you want your business's advocacy function to become once it has matured.

The answer is likely to depend on the type of business you operate, how large your company is, and how central third-party developers are to your business model. If you're a startup, it probably makes sense to limit the focus of your developer advocacy initiatives to creating a small team of content producers who raise awareness of your organization within developer communities but who don't do much more until your company becomes larger (or gets acquired by a larger company that has its own developer advocacy function). This type of developer advocacy program will help to get your business off the ground and establish brand recognition in a market where most third-party developers are not yet aware of what your company even offers.

In contrast, for larger businesses with established brands, the goal of the developer advocacy function is typically to sustain a relatively large team – one that consists of at least a half-dozen advocates – that engages with third-party developer communities in diverse ways that include but are not limited to producing content. The advocates might also appear at conferences, collaborate with third-party developers on building integrations, and help to bring the voices of third-party developers to bear on the business's conversations surrounding the evolution of its own products.

Companies where public APIs or tooling serve as the lifeblood of the business — a strategy typically known as being "Developer First" — are likely to set different goals than those that offer APIs or integrations to third-party developers. A good contrast here is between Salesforce and Amazon Web Services (AWS). Salesforce's product suite would be of little value for most consumers without the integrations created by third-party programmers. Meanwhile, AWS benefits from a good relationship with third-party developers who use its products and who in many cases create applications that depend on those products. But AWS's core business model does not depend on third-party extensions of or integrations with its offerings; it depends only on ensuring that customers use its cloud services.

For a business like Salesforce, then, creating a developer advocacy function that keeps third-party developers constantly aware of new API offerings and integration opportunities is absolutely vital. Salesforce might therefore create a larger, more dynamic developer advocacy program that is capable of promoting its entire ecosystem of offerings. In contrast, for a company like AWS, the developer advocacy program is likely to be somewhat smaller and limited to promoting good relations with developers who are customers of the business's services, as opposed to those who want to create unique integrations with AWS's APIs or platform.

Approaches to Structuring an Advocacy Team

Once you set goals for what your advocacy program is supposed to achieve, you can plan a team structure that aligns with those goals. The structure is important because it defines whom developer advocates work alongside and answer to. By extension, the structure serves as a framework that governs how advocacy will fit within your broader business as it evolves from a one-person experiment to a mature business function.

As with most other aspects of developer advocacy, there is no "one right way" to structure the program. Instead, there are multiple viable approaches.

Advocacy As a Part of Product Development

In the opinion of the authors of this book, the best way to structure a developer advocacy program is to have advocates work under the auspices of the business's product management unit.

There are two key advantages to this approach. One is that product development is an unusual business function in that it has both a technical and a marketing focus. In this sense, product development is a natural fit for advocates, who also need to understand both the technical aspects of what their business offers and market demands.

The second advantage of using product development to structure advocacy is that product developers stand to benefit most from sustained engagement with third-party developers. By serving as a conduit through which the product developers can share ideas with – and receive feedback from – external developer communities, developer advocates can guide the way products evolve, thereby bringing enormous value to product development work. Other business functions may benefit indirectly from the work of developer advocates, but few enjoy such direct benefits.

That said, structuring advocates as part of the product development function is not without risks or downsides. One challenge to be aware of is the chance that, because the product development unit within the business is itself structured in terms of different product offerings or types of functionality, different advocates may become aligned with different products, areas of functionality, or business domains. This leads to siloed advocacy programs where each advocate specializes in advocating for a different offering or engages with a different community; as a result, advocacy success within each silo becomes dependent on the efforts of a single individual, leading to the scalability and turnover problems of single-member advocacy programs.

The siloing of advocacy programs and teams can be unavoidable for larger organizations that have multiple offerings, or whose platforms include complex functionality that is difficult for an entire advocacy team to represent collectively. However, smaller organizations should ensure that advocacy responsibilities are shared across products or areas of functionality in order to avoid siloing. And if siloing can't be avoided, teams should at least make an effort to assign multiple developers to each product or offering so that there are no advocates operating effectively as single-person teams.

Another risk is that if the boundaries between advocacy and product management are not well defined, advocates may end up stepping on the toes of product developers, and vice versa. For example, advocates may believe that they should be helping to chart the evolution of a product (which is not a primary function of developer advocacy) in addition to engaging with third-party developers. As a result, advocates and product developers can end up working at cross-purposes or competing for resources, rather than collaborating toward common goals. This challenge can be mitigated by clearly defining where advocates fit within product development and what advocates should and should not be doing with regard to product development work.

Advocates As Product Marketers

Another approach to structuring developer advocacy – and the most common one – is to have developer advocates work within the product marketing unit. The main advantage of this strategy is that it allows advocates to contribute to the messaging aspects of product marketers.

However, there are major downsides of making advocacy part of product marketing. Arguably the greatest is that this approach makes it hard to distinguish the work of advocates from the work of marketers. Advocacy risks becoming rolled up in broader marketing initiatives that water down the unique value that advocates can bring to the organization. In the worst cases, advocates end up being treated as generic marketers, with their value measured using metrics like total leads generated – a poor way of quantifying what advocates do, since the purpose of advocates is not to create and nurture leads but rather to build strong ties with external developer communities, even if those ties don't directly translate to closed deals or revenue.

Thus, while it may seem to make sense initially to structure advocacy as part of product marketing, doing so is generally not a best practice. The only common exception is if your business is a small startup that does not yet have a mature product development function; in that case, organizing advocates alongside product marketers makes more sense.

Engineering As a Home for Advocates

Another strategy we commonly see in startups that launch developer advocacy programs is to make advocates part of the engineering organization. This strategy allows advocates to maintain very close ties with technical leads and to focus on creating technical content – which is beneficial for startups whose main goal with regard to external communities is simply to build awareness.

Organizing advocacy as part of engineering also offers the advantage of shielding advocates from the go-to-market side of product management, which can be hamstring advocates' work within startups because new businesses often experiment with multiple go-to-market strategies as they mature. In contrast, engineering tends to be a more stable function, allowing advocates to contribute in a more consistent way.

The chief disadvantage of making advocacy a part of engineering is that it increases the risk that advocates will be funneled into performing technical support, which (as we explained in Chapter 1 and as we discuss again in the following section) should not be the purpose of advocacy programs. There is also a risk that engineering teams will task advocates with completing work that engineers don't want to do, like writing documentation.

Treating Developers As Support Specialists

Another seemingly obvious way to structure advocacy teams is to make them part of the business's technical support function. This may appear to make sense given that advocates have a deep understanding of and empathy with the challenges that external developers face when using a business's platform. They can give third-party users direct architectural advice and answer complex questions that generic support staff may not always be able to address.

However, it is typically not a best practice to treat advocacy as part of technical support. Doing so is very likely to result in an advocacy team that ends up being treated as an elite support unit and nothing more. Instead of focusing on broad engagement with external developer communities, advocates end up spending their days resolving support requests, which quickly saps advocacy programs of the bulk of their value. It also turns advocacy work into a relatively monotonous, tedious function, leading to challenges in hiring and retaining skilled advocates.

Choosing a Structure

As we've noted, organizing advocacy under the banner of product development typically makes the most sense. That said, it's important to consider your overall business size and structure, as well as the types of external developer communities you need to engage, in order to decide where advocates can best fit.

For instance, as we mentioned, a startup may find that it makes more sense to treat advocacy as an extension of engineering, for the simple reason that other business functions are not as well established at smaller startups. Likewise, a business whose platform is partly or fully open source, and which therefore wishes to attract third-party developers not only to use its platform but also to help build it, may benefit more from having advocates work alongside engineers than would a business whose product is proprietary. The reason why is that as part of the engineering team, advocates can help to turn external developers into contributors – something that would not happen in businesses where the platform is built only by internal developers.

Note, too, that it's possible to adopt a hybrid structure in which developer advocates are attached to multiple units within the business. For instance, some advocates may work as part of the product development team, while others work alongside engineers. This cross-functional approach allows each advocate to contribute in ways that offer the most value based on their particular interests or areas of expertise.

That said, a hybrid advocacy program can be difficult to manage, and it may lead to a highly siloed advocacy operation. Before endeavoring to create an advocacy team that spans multiple units of the business, create a mature advocacy program within one business function, and scale it up from there. Only highly mature advocacy programs should attempt to become cross-functional.

Planning Advocacy Operations

In addition to planning how to structure your advocacy team within the broader business, you must decide what you want your advocates to do once the program is fully operational. There are two main components of advocacy work – external and internal – and although almost all advocacy teams do both, the way they divide up their time and effort should vary depending on your business's priorities.

External Advocacy: The Bread and Butter of Advocacy Work

External advocacy – meaning engagement with third-party developer communities who are external to the business – is the core focus of most advocacy teams. In general, it accounts for 50 to 70 percent of advocates' time and effort.

External engagement activities typically include the following:

- Having open-ended conversations with relevant external developer audiences – including those already using the business's platform and those who may use it in the future. Conversations can range from direct discussions of the platform to product-agnostic discussions of topics like career goals or general banter. The goal of these conversations is to create and nurture engagement with external developers, regardless of the specific focus.

- Creating content, such as blogs, webinars, tutorials, videos, and in-person presentations at events like developer conferences. Content is key to external developer advocacy because it serves as the foundation upon which many conversations with third-party developers take place. In addition, it provides an opportunity to showcase the business's platform and display examples of how external developers can use it.

In the course of pursuing both of these external advocacy activities, it's critical for advocates to focus on being authentic in their engagement with third-party developers. In other words, advocates must avoid the appearance of pushing a specific marketing agenda or engaging external developer communities for the pure purpose of generating revenue. Instead, they should engage for engagement's own sake.

The best way to achieve authentic engagement is to know what external developers expect and want. The external component of advocacy programs should therefore be tailored to the specific personas that businesses want to reach within external developer communities. For instance, if relevant external developers are highly active on a particular social media platform, that should be a center of engagement. If they prefer reading blogs to watching videos, that should inform the focus of external advocacy. Choosing the right engagement strategy and approach goes a long way toward creating a highly authentic external advocacy operation that genuinely appeals to external audiences.

Along related lines, although individual advocates may have preferred modes and platforms for external engagement, they'll ideally be assigned a mix, rather than operating in a specific way. In other words, you don't want one advocate to operate solely on YouTube as a means of external engagement while another specializes in creating and sharing content on Discord. Instead, advocates should work across multiple media and engage with communities in multiple ways, based on objectives related to engagement and audience building that are set on a regular basis – such as once a quarter.

Internal Advocacy: Bringing Unique Perspective to Internal Stakeholders

While engaging with external developer communities is the main focus of advocates, advocacy operations should also extend to internal audiences via what we call internal advocacy. Internal advocacy happens when the advocacy team engages with product, engineering, and marketing teams within the business (even if the advocates are not structured within these teams) in order to provide feedback, cultivate messaging, and so on.

Internal advocacy isn't always easy, due especially to the fact that internal groups are not often inclined to look to advocates for guidance. Product marketers, engineers, and so on have a tendency to assume they already have the answers they need. They may not prove particularly warm toward what they view as unsolicited advice from advocates.

However, the reality is that, due to their engagement with external audiences, advocates have a unique perspective that allows them to provide nuanced feedback that is hard to achieve via other channels (like market research). In this way, internal advocacy can create value for the business via practices like the following:

- **Feedback to product teams:** Advocates should be a regular part of internal conversations among product teams about future product development. Advocates understand better than anyone else how external developers are using products and what they expect from products, so their feedback is critical for ensuring that product road maps actually meet the needs of target audiences.

- **Feedback to engineering:** Advocates can advise engineers on how external developers are using their product, which technical issues they are experiencing, how they are working around shortcomings, and how the core product could be improved from the perspective of external users. At the same time, engaging with the business's engineers provides advocates with more perspective on and technical knowledge of the product, further enhancing their ability to engage with external audiences.

- **Marketing guidance:** For any business with a software platform that engages third-party coders, it's imperative for marketing teams to deliver messaging and drive marketing campaigns that meet the expectations of those developers. But this can be challenging for marketers to do alone due to their lack of both technical expertise and opportunities to interface directly with developers. By filling each of these gaps, advocates can work internally to provide critical guidance to marketing teams. Advocates can, for example, help to plan and review marketing content and tweak messaging to ensure it aligns with the specific expectations of external developers.

- **Feedback for business leaders:** Because advocates have a deep understanding of the technical ecosystem in which a business operates, as well as of external communities that depend on the business's products, they are in a unique position to offer valuable perspective on high-level business decisions. They can advise executives on go-to-market strategies for new products, for instance, and offer feedback on potential acquisition plans. Although this type of internal advocacy work is not typically a primary focus for advocates, occasional engagement by advocates with high-level decision-makers at the business can create tremendous value for guiding the overall direction of the company.

Importantly, advocates shouldn't be pushed into "owning" any of the internal advocacy roles described previously. In other words, and as we've stated previously, advocates shouldn't be treated as a special type of product manager, engineer, marketer, and so on. Instead, advocates must occupy a distinct role (and one that, again, focuses primarily on external advocacy), even as they work closely with other business units to provide vital internal guidance. Decisions about matters like product development and marketing must ultimately be made by the parts of the organization that own those functions, not advocates, although advocates should be able to offer advice about such decisions.

Scaling Advocacy Programs

In many ways, starting an advocacy program by identifying one or a few individuals who want to take on an advocacy role is the easy part. The real challenge lies in scaling the program so that it includes enough advocates to fulfill the complete set of external and internal advocacy requirements described previously. At the same time, scaling up is important to ensure that the business does not become dependent on just one or a handful of individual advocates whose departure from the company would lead to the disintegration of the advocacy program.

Successful scaling requires a systematic approach to hiring and retaining advocates, as well as a way to structure the advocacy such that it can operate cohesively as it grows.

Hiring

Hiring advocates can be challenging, not least due to the small size of the developer advocate and developer relations markets. Partly for that reason, it's wise to expand advocate job searches beyond the small pool of individuals currently working in advocacy or a closely related role.

Instead, businesses should hire advocates based on attributes, not previous advocacy experience. If candidates have the attributes described in Chapter 2 – such as technical experience, a passion for communicating with developers, and an established point of view about a technical ecosystem or platform – they are strong candidates for advocacy roles. Hiring managers or recruiters in charge of leading searches for developer advocates should actively seek out individuals who have the right attributes for advocacy but who may never have considered applying for an advocacy role.

After identifying candidates and starting the application review process, hiring managers should carefully review written application materials to gain a sense of just how skilled advocates are in telling stories and demonstrating passion for engaging technical communities. Reviewing publicly available content, such as blog posts and videos, that candidates have produced is another valuable means of vetting applicants. (If a candidate has no publicly available content, that could be a red flag, although it's possible that candidates for entry-level advocacy positions will not yet have established themselves as content producers and thought leaders within a technical community even if they have strong potential to do so.)

At the interview stage, too, hiring managers and committees should be on the lookout for proof of the specific skills that make for a successful advocate. Consider requiring candidates to give a presentation as part of the interview in order to vet their storytelling skills and evaluate their ability to discuss technical content in an engaging, passionate, and empathetic manner. Be sure as well to ask questions that assess how well candidates understand the way that different business units – like product management, engineering, and marketing – work and how they can contribute to them as advocates while also retaining a distinct identity. Questioning the views of candidates a bit can be helpful, too, as a means of evaluating how empathetic they are in response to criticism.

Ultimately, the goal of the hiring process should be to find and validate candidates who can deliver the unique blend of technical skills, passion for communication, and business sense that drive a successful advocacy function. Previous work experience is less important for advocacy applicants than it is for other types of roles.

Compensation

Successful hiring, as well as successful retention, of advocates hinges in large part on offering adequate compensation. But deciding how much salary to pay to advocates can be difficult given the novelty of the role at many businesses.

Although compensation norms for advocates are evolving rapidly as advocacy roles become more common at businesses (and as the technology industry as a whole reacts to changing financial and labor trends), our research shows that standard salary ranges for advocates at present are as follows:

- Associate advocate: $90,000–130,000

- Advocate: $110,000–150,000

- Senior advocate: $130,000–180,000

- Principal advocate: $150,000–220,000

- Lead advocate: $150,000–200,000

- Advocacy leadership: 220+

The range has been shown to vary wildly based on key factors of technical experience, region, and size of company (*source: Independent Research + Common Room 2022 Compensation Report*).

We explain what the various roles of advocates mean in the following subsection.

In addition to these figures, businesses can use product management salaries to gain perspective on how much compensation to offer advocates. Product management roles at varying levels (associate, senior, manager, and so on) align relatively closely compensation-wise with advocacy roles at the same levels.

Defining Roles

A scalable advocacy program needs to include multiple roles, each corresponding to different levels of experience.

Currently, businesses with mature advocacy programs maintain the following roles:

- **Associate advocate:** An entry-level advocacy position. Ideal for individuals who are relatively new to the technology industry and do not yet have specific advocacy experience but who have a passion and talent for communication with software developers.

- **Advocate:** A role for advocates with at least basic experience communicating with developers, even if they have not previously done so in a formal advocacy role.

- **Senior advocate:** Senior advocates should already have an established reputation in technical communities and a demonstrated ability to communicate with developers via multiple channels. They should also have a strong sense of how advocacy serves the business and how they can use internal advocacy to bring value to specific business units.

- **Principal advocate:** An experienced advocate and sought-after technical expert committed to advocacy as a long-term career path. Principal advocates do not aspire to move into a director-level or higher business position but instead seek to engage with developer communities on an ongoing basis while leveraging that experience to bring value to the business in multiple ways.

- **Lead advocate:** A seasoned advocate who understands not just what advocates do and how they contribute to the business but who is able to manage other advocates and lead continued growth of the advocacy function.

- **Advocacy leadership:** A high-level role that requires extensive management experience. Advocacy experience is also important, but because directors of advocacy are not engaged with developer communities on a day-to-day basis, the best advocates are not necessarily the best advocacy directors, and vice versa.

Not all advocacy programs require all of these roles. Indeed, it's not until businesses establish relatively large, relatively mature advocacy programs – ones that include at least about ten individual associate advocates, advocates, or senior advocates – that they typically begin creating higher-level advocacy roles. However, eventually establishing all of these roles is important in order to create a fully mature, systemic advocacy program.

Conclusion

This chapter has detailed how to launch, grow, and sustain an advocacy program at your business. We've also touched on what advocates should do once they become a part of your business, but we discussed that topic mostly in the context of how developers can interface with other parts of the business.

In the next two chapters, we'll dive deeper into the type of work advocates should perform on a day-to-day basis – such as which specific tasks businesses should assign to advocates and how advocates should manage content programs.

So, if you're wondering exactly what to expect of your advocates once you've established them, read on.

Managing Work Output for Your New Advocacy Team

The previous chapter discussed how to create a developer advocacy team. But what do you do with your developer advocates (or if you're just starting out, your single advocate) once you've introduced the function into your business. In other words, which work expectations should you set for advocates, how should you structure their tasks, and how do you measure their success?

Those are the questions we tackle in this chapter, which is geared for organizations that are in the process of starting advocacy programs. It provides specific guidance on what managers, executives, and advocates themselves should expect their advocacy teams to be doing and how to assess the extent to which advocate work aligns with business needs and goals.

© Chris Riley, Chris Tozzi 2023
C. Riley and C. Tozzi, *Developer Advocacy*,
https://doi.org/10.1007/978-1-4842-9597-7_4

Developer Advocacy Work: A Category-by-Category Breakdown

At a high level, advocacy work can be broken down into two main categories: external and internal advocacy operations. There's also a third category of work, called growth and operations, that advocates sometimes need to handle.

Let's look at each category of advocacy work and which specific tasks and responsibilities it entails.

External Advocacy Work

As we explained in earlier chapters, external advocacy is typically the main focus of advocacy programs. We estimate that, in general, external advocacy accounts for about 60 percent of the total work effort of successful advocacy teams.

Key tasks in external advocacy work include the following:

- Engaging with outside developers who constitute the developer communities with which the business seeks to build strong relationships. Engagement work can take place in private spaces, such as private Slack channels or in-person workshops in which external developers participate. Engagement can also happen in public arenas like social media. Indeed, it should happen in both contexts, because private engagement allows advocates to work with developers in greater depth and with more focus than they can typically achieve in spaces like social media, while public engagement offers the benefit of more effectively demonstrating advocates' commitment to developer communities.

- Developing a content, such as blog posts and videos, that helps support external developer communities. As we explain in greater depth in the next chapter, content should be designed to provide organic, intrinsic value to developers based on their needs and interests. It should also align with specific goals; advocates shouldn't spend time creating content just to create content, but rather to work toward a clear objective — such as helping external developers learn how to take advantage of a new product feature.

- Developing a point of view. As we've stated, it's important for advocates to have opinions, especially about technical matters that interest external developer communities. Developing informed opinions takes time, and so part of the work required to perform external advocacy is doing the research and analysis necessary to create meaningful opinions.

- Cultivating personal brands. Even though advocates primarily represent the business when they engage with external communities, their work is more credible to external audiences – and their careers are likely to be more enjoyable – when they are also given space to develop interests and pursue accomplishments that round them out as more than just advocates. For example, an advocate who comes from a programming background might work on a personal open source project that's not directly related to their advocacy work but which informs and supports it. Businesses should factor this type of "personal" labor into the external engagement work that advocates perform.

When advocates perform these tasks on a regular basis, they can sustain effective and meaningful engagement with external developer communities.

Internal Advocacy

Internal advocacy should represent only a minority of the total work that advocates perform – 30 percent of total effort is a healthy figure to target – but it's nonetheless an essential component of advocacy operations. Internal advocacy, as we explained in Chapter 3, is the work by which advocates represent external developer personas to stakeholders inside the business, such as product managers, engineers, and marketers, so that external developers' needs will inform important technical and business decisions.

Internal advocacy work is in some ways the most difficult type of advocacy work to perform – not because it takes more time overall (it doesn't), but because it often requires navigating internal organizational politics and structures. As a result, it's difficult to chart a one-size-fits-all approach to organizing internal advocacy, but the main focus should be to ensure that advocates engage on a regular basis with internal stakeholders.

In practice, this might mean that advocates take part in product management meetings, for example, or that they have visibility into internal engineering discussions about product feature development.

When internal advocacy is successful, stakeholders from across the business view advocates as a trusted source of guidance that can inform the various decisions they have to make. If it's unsuccessful, there is no systematic feedback loop that ensures that external developer needs are considered when the business makes decisions internally. Or feedback occasionally happens, but it comes too late – after product development, marketing, or messaging decisions have already been made and implemented, and it's very difficult or impossible to adjust in response to feedback from advocates who recognize the needs of external developer communities.

Growth and Operations

Growth and operations work is the effort that the advocacy team spends evaluating its current status, planning new projects, and finding ways to scale and grow. This type of labor is easy to overlook, but it's critical for ensuring that the team as a whole can grow and scale effectively.

That's especially true given that advocates tend to perform external and internal engagement work individually, which means that each advocate tends to have limited visibility into what other advocates are doing or how they can coordinate their efforts. By making growth and operations work a formal part of overall advocacy work, businesses help to ensure that their advocacy teams are able to set aside the time and effort necessary to coordinate and scale operations effectively – and, in turn, that advocacy delivers maximum value to the organization. On the whole, about 10 percent of total advocacy effort should be devoted to growth and operations.

The exact tasks involved in advocacy growth and operations work vary depending on the needs of the team at any given moment in time. But in general, the focus of this type of work should be on identifying ways for developers to coordinate their efforts and support each other as effectively as possible, in the contexts of both external and internal advocacy.

For example, as part of growth and operations work that advances internal advocacy initiatives, advocates might share information about which types of feedback they've shared with internal stakeholders so that the team as a whole has visibility into the internal guidance its members have offered. From there, advocates might plan strategies to hold stakeholders accountable for following up on advice they agreed to take. In this way, advocacy teams coordinate their efforts to ensure that internal advocacy has an actual effect and does not amount to mere ideas that stakeholders never act upon.

As another example of growth and operations work, advocates might meet to review recent content achievements and then decide how they can share and repurpose content with each other. This type of coordination amplifies the impact of content while also using advocate resources more effectively.

Without devoting some time to coordinating content operations, one advocate might end up with redundant content that another has already produced. It's also difficult to ensure that different content examples complement each other and work toward shared, team-wide goals – as opposed to the goals and interests of individual advocates only.

An additional focus of growth and operations should be measuring and reporting on the success of developer advocacy operations. We explained in Chapter 1 how the business as a whole can assess advocacy's impact and which metrics to track, so we won't cover that material again here. But what is important to state is that it's critical for advocates to work together when deciding how to assess their work's impact and share the impact with the business.

Otherwise, the advocacy team ends up losing control of its destiny because other stakeholders within the business are left to interpret advocacy's impact in whichever ways make sense to them – which many will struggle to do because they are not very familiar with the concept of advocacy and have little or no experience in evaluating its contributions to the business. Alternatively, without measurement coordination by the advocacy team, business stakeholders will focus on assessing the work performed by individual advocates, without appreciating the impact of the advocacy function as a whole.

When advocates coordinate reporting efforts, however, they are in a stronger position to communicate the impact of their work and share data that might otherwise be overlooked. They can also show how the contributions of each individual add up to create an overall impact on the business that is (in many cases) greater than the sum of its parts, given the ways in which individual advocacy initiatives complement and amplify each other. There may, of course, be disagreement within the advocacy team about how to measure and report on impact, but it's better to have explicit conversations about this and reach a consensus than to ignore the importance of measurement as one facet of operations and growth work.

Advocacy Work Processes

Previously, we explained which types of tasks advocates should perform. Now, let's look at which work processes and related resources the business must implement to ensure that advocates can operate effectively.

Advocacy Services Menu

Ideally, advocates should be available upon request to perform services for other parts of the business. In order to facilitate this process, businesses should implement a "services menu" that describes what advocates can do and how to request that they do it.

Offering a list of available services is important because many other stakeholders inside the business may be unaware of everything that advocates can offer. In particular, they may not realize that advocates are available to help with internal processes like product management and marketing.

By establishing a formal list of services and a process for requesting those services, businesses make it easy for all stakeholders to leverage advocacy in a proactive way. Otherwise, they may be stuck in a state where advocates are brought in reactively to solve problems (such as issues that arise when external developers don't know how to use a new product feature) but are not part of these processes from the start.

In addition, an advocacy services menu helps to define what advocates *don't* do. For example, it can help to avoid expectations that advocates will write documentation or handle customer support requests on a routine basis – tasks that, as we explained earlier, should not be the focus of advocates.

Wikis and Newsletters

To reinforce understanding within the business of which services advocates offer and how to access them, consider creating internally available wikis, newsletters, or similar resources. These resources provide another means of making stakeholders aware of what advocates can do, and using these types of media, it's possible to provide more context and share examples than you could include in an advocacy services menu.

The bottom line here is that it's worth investing in internal resources that describe how stakeholders inside your business can benefit from advocates, in addition to listing the specific services that advocates offer.

External Engagement Platforms

For the purposes of external engagement, advocates need platforms they can work from. In this context, a platform could be any type of physical or virtual space where advocates can engage with external developers.

Some engagement platforms, such as open source projects that interest developers relevant to your business's brand, may already exist and be controlled by third parties. But others will need to be implemented explicitly.

For example, you might decide to launch your own open source project to provide a place where your advocates can engage with third-party developers. Or you might develop a presence on a specific social media platform that is relevant to the developers your advocates want to engage with.

When selecting which platforms to target, it's important to recognize your advocates' operational limits. There are almost always more platforms available than there are platforms that they can feasibly operate on, and you want to avoid having your advocacy teams become overstretched because they are trying to be in too many places at once. As a rule, it's better to have a heavy presence on relatively few platforms than to try to operate across too many platforms and have a weak or superficial presence on some of them. You don't want to launch an open source project only to have it stagnate, for example. That would undercut the goals of external advocacy because it would make your brand appear less dynamic and engaging to outside developers.

So, when selecting platforms, think about which ones are likely to be most useful for engaging with external audiences. Think, too, about the individual skill sets and public profiles of each advocate on your team, and align those with the platforms you choose to leverage.

Finally, be sure when selecting platforms to know how you will track engagement. Your metrics will necessarily vary from one platform to another – in an open source project, for instance, you might track how many contributors you have or how many code commits they make, whereas on social media, you could track how much engagement your advocates' content receives – but the important thing is to ensure you are systematically measuring the effectiveness of each platform as a vehicle for engaging with your target external developer communities. Ideally, your measurement will allow you to assess not just raw engagement but also the depth and meaningfulness of engagement; for instance, rather than counting crude metrics like how many times developers read an advocate's blog post, you might go deeper by measuring how many substantive comments it receives or how many times it's cited in other posts written by external developers.

Social Presence and Management

In almost all cases, social media services will represent some of the platforms where your advocates operate. To leverage social media effectively as a pillar of developer advocacy, it's important to have a management strategy.

You should decide who controls your advocates' access to social platforms, as well as when and where advocates share content on social media. Determining how frequently they engage is important too – and remember that there may sometimes be periods where engagement activity should spike because, for instance, an event in the news creates a focus on your business by external developers, or you've released a new product or feature relevant to them. In other words, your social engagement strategy should be flexible enough to accommodate shifting, and sometimes unpredictable, business priorities; strategies like "we post once per day at 9 a.m." are not dynamic enough to drive maximum external advocacy results.

A final element of social management to consider is how your advocates present themselves within social media settings. Will they operate using personal accounts, using official accounts associated with your business, or both? The answer may vary across social platforms (indeed, not all platforms make it possible to link accounts officially to a business), but this is an important question to consider because it affects the way your advocates are perceived and how closely external audiences associate them with your brand.

Content Management

We detail content management strategies for advocates in the following chapter. But for now, let us note that it's critical to ensure that advocacy teams have the resources they need to curate topics for content, create the content, review the content internally, and publish the content in places where it will reach developer audiences. From there, content should be tracked in order to measure and respond to engagement.

In other words, good content doesn't happen automatically. It requires tools like project management systems (for planning and developing content), content management systems (for publishing content), and a means of monitoring content once it is in the wild.

Planning and Review Framework

To ensure that advocacy efforts are regularly assessed and reviewed and to help facilitate the growth and operations work described previously, businesses should develop a planning and review framework that details when and how the advocacy team meets to evaluate its operations and plan for continuous improvement. In general, these formal meetings take place once a quarter.

In addition to defining how often advocacy team reviews take place, the planning and review framework should detail the metrics and other measurement methods used to assess the performance of both individual advocates and the team as a whole. By spelling out this information in a formal way, businesses help to set clear goals that advocates can work toward. They also expedite reviews and make it easier to find opportunities for improving advocacy operations.

Conclusion

We explained in this chapter how to organize developer advocacy work and effort. Admittedly, the varied nature of advocacy operations means that there is no singular, clear-cut recipe to follow in this regard, but there are overarching goals that should guide the way businesses approach the structuring of advocacy labor. There are also guidelines for ensuring that advocates have the resources they need to perform their work well and to review that work and align it with business goals.

In the next chapter, we'll extend the discussion of implementing developer advocacy operations by diving into content and the role it plays in effective advocacy in more detail.

Getting Started with Content for Developer Advocacy

The previous chapter touched on the role content plays in advocacy work. But content is so central to effective advocacy that it deserves a chapter of its own. Indeed, it's not a stretch to say that content is the foundation of advocacy. It's the platform that all other advocacy work – internal and external – branches off of.

> Developer content is important for education and awareness. Developers need to have the confidence they can do what they want with your product. They need self serve help, so they can learn on their own. That is why things like how-to's need to exist and be easily accessible. You must understand what their friction points are as a marketer, because developers move fast and are very capable, don't get in their way.
>
> —Sara Rosso, Technical Marketing Leader

© Chris Riley, Chris Tozzi 2023
C. Riley and C. Tozzi, *Developer Advocacy*,
https://doi.org/10.1007/978-1-4842-9597-7_5

Content is also a particularly complex type of advocacy resource. On the surface, using content to advance advocacy may seem simple enough: You tell your advocates to produce content, they do so, and your business naturally experiences a huge positive impact, right? Not exactly. There are a number of variables at play in effective content operations – such as which types of content to produce, how to distribute it, and how to measure its impact, to name just a few of the decisions your advocacy team will need to make when executing its content strategy – and you need a systematic approach to content management in order to decide how to run a successful content strategy.

Content for advocates can also be difficult to plan, execute, and assess because businesses may mistakenly assume that they can borrow from content marketers' playbooks. In marketing, content has long been used to generate leads and increase customer engagement. However, the reality is that advocates have different goals from marketers, and content strategies that work for marketing purposes only sometimes align with those that work in the context of advocacy. If advocates think like content marketers when formulating content strategy, their efforts are likely to deliver few desired results.

To provide guidance on how advocates should think and operate with regard to content, this chapter walks through everything that business stakeholders and advocates themselves need to know about the role of content in developer advocacy. It explains how content supports advocacy, which characteristics help ensure the success of content, and how to measure the impact of content. It also lays out the processes necessary to produce effective content on a reliable basis, and it highlights some of the common antipatterns and mistakes advocates run into when working with content – such as having unrealistic expectations about content's ability to "go viral."

The Role of Content in Developer Advocacy

The reason why content is so central to developer advocacy is simple: content is one of the most effective mediums through which advocates can engage external developer audiences. In some cases, content can also advance internal advocacy initiatives by helping advocates to communicate and share their points of view with stakeholders inside the business.

It's certainly possible, of course, to engage with target audiences without content. An advocate could go and approach individual developers at a conference to chat with them, for instance, or sit in on internal meetings to perform internal advocacy work. But these engagement efforts are difficult to scale. They also are not excellent ways of drawing audience interest.

Content, on the other hand, lends itself well to scalable advocacy operations. A single piece of content – such as a blog post or video – could engage tens of thousands of individuals in some cases. Many forms of content also enable continuous, ongoing engagement because target audiences can consume content at any time and on an indefinite basis. That makes content much more efficient and scalable than forms of engagement that require advocates to interface with stakeholders one-on-one.

At the same time, well-planned and executed content is intrinsically engaging to target audiences. As a result, rather than having to beg for developers' attention, content allows advocates to secure their voluntary and organic attention. This approach lays the foundation for more meaningful engagement and for building stronger, more durable relationships.

A third advantage of content from the perspective of advocates is that content is a great way of sharing a brand's point of view or messaging without coming off as heavy-handed or explicitly promotional. In contrast to, say, marketing material, technical content that helps developers solve a problem or think in a new way is much more likely to be taken seriously by the audiences it reaches. It feels less threatening than explicitly promotional messaging, allowing it to make a deeper and more enduring impact on developers.

So, while producing content is only one facet of advocacy operations, it's arguably the single most important work that advocates perform.

Steps in a Content Strategy

To produce effective content that drives meaningful engagement with technical audiences, advocates need a systematic content strategy in place. That strategy should include several discrete steps: curation, development, review, publication, and measurement.

Curation

Curation is the process through which advocates plan content. Curation is critical because no matter how well executed content is, it's unlikely to make much of a dent in the minds of developers if the content deals with topics they are not interested in or is delivered in a form they won't consume.

Successful curation, then, starts with knowing your audience. To this end, it's helpful to think in terms of which personas exist within your developer communities. Which types of work do they do? Which technologies do they use? Which problems or challenges do they care most about? Which types of media do they consume? You can't curate content effectively until you can answer these questions.

Fortunately, these questions should be easy for a good advocate to answer because advocates spend the bulk of their time working within the developer communities they support. If your advocates don't already have a sense of what their target personas are, they should be able to gain one easily enough by simply asking the developers questions like those outlined in the preceding paragraph.

Keep in mind that it's crucial to be as specific as possible when evaluating developer personas. Generic persona descriptions like "we target front-end developers" are not very helpful because they are not pointed enough. A better persona type to focus on would be "front-end developers who specialize in AngularJS for mobile apps and who use CI/CD development practices." Remember, too, that it's likely that there are multiple types of personas within the developer communities you seek to engage with.

Once you know your personas, you can decide which content angles will best reach them. There are four main categories to consider:

- **Thought leadership:** Thought leadership content aims to be eye-opening and to teach content consumers new ways of thinking about old problems. The content doesn't have to be overly technical – it need not get down into the code level, for example – but it should deal with technical issues that the target audience cares about.

- **Purely technical:** Purely technical content includes pieces like tutorials or how-to articles. It focuses explicitly and in depth on a specific technical process, with the goal of helping consumers learn to do something new or solve a problem.

- **Educational:** Educational content informs consumers. Its technical depth can vary depending on the topic in question, but unlike purely technical content, educational content's purpose is not to show an audience *how* to do something. Instead, it's focused on the *why* and *what*. It's also different from thought leadership because it doesn't deal with a totally original or pathbreaking idea or concept; instead, it focuses on nuts-and-bolts information that matters to the target audience.

- **Decision-making:** Decision-making content helps developers make important decisions. Buyer's guides that compare different solutions are an example. So are articles that compare one way of doing something (like CI/CD) to another (like waterfall-style software delivery).

In most cases, advocacy teams will use a combination of multiple content dimensions within their content strategies. But the weighting afforded to each type should reflect the needs and desires of developer communities. Personas that care more about being shown how to do something, for example, will benefit from purely technical content more than developers who are most interested in innovative high-level thinking of the type offered by thought leadership content. Likewise, developers who play a role in tool purchasing decisions will appreciate decision-making content more than those looking for technical tutorials on how to use a tool.

The curation process must also include decisions about which types of content to create. Common examples include

- Blog posts
- Videos
- Tutorials
- White papers
- Ebooks
- Webinars
- Conference presentations

Here again, content type should align with developer personas. Advocates should consider which types of content their target audiences consume most often and which media channels they are most active in.

Remember, too, that it's often possible to repurpose the same content across multiple formats. A blog post that provides an introduction to a new tool could be expanded into a tutorial that shows how to use the tool, for example, while a webinar could offer a live demonstration of using the tool. During the curation process, advocates should be on the lookout for ways to get the most bang out of their content ideas and development effort.

Development

Once advocates have decided which dimensions and topics to focus on in content, as well as which specific types of content to create, they can begin the content development process.

The exact nature of this process will vary depending on the nature of the content. But in general, priorities to bear in mind include the following:

- Be clear and keep it simple. The less work your audience has to do to understand what you're trying to say, the better. Avoid rhetorical flourishes and complex lead-ins unless they add real value to a piece. In general, it's better for content to be simple and easy to digest than to be flashy and hard for readers to understand.

- Have a point of view. Content that is compelling is driven by a point of view. Even if you're developing educational or purely technical content, it should be clear to the reader that you have opinions about best practices or ideal solutions to technical issues. Content that lacks a point of view or central argument is more forgettable. It also makes the author look less credible.

- Focus on a clear audience problem. You should be sure during the curation process to choose content topics that your audience cares about, but don't forget that priority during content development. Advocates must focus on delivering information that their audience cares about – even if it's not necessarily the same as what the business cares about.

- Avoid promotion. In general, the best content is very light on explicit brand promotion. In many cases, it doesn't promote a brand or brand message at all. Advocates shouldn't mention their businesses or products unless there is a clear technical reason to do so – and they should resist pressure from internal stakeholders to be overly promotional. The purpose of content in the context of advocacy is not the same as marketing or sales content, and advocates must keep this in mind at every point of the content development process.

- Keep it short. In most cases, less is more when it comes to content. Developers are more likely to read or view content if it's shorter. Content should therefore be concise and straight to the point. Long contextual stories or tangential discussions may be interesting for content authors to share, but they rarely add value to content from the audience's perspective.

- Keep it modular. Never assume the audience will actually read or watch content in its entirety. Instead, make it easy for developers to skim content by breaking it into sections. Content that is not modular is more likely to be ignored by developers who don't want to commit the time to reading or viewing all sections.

- Keep the message obvious. Because some consumers will skim through content, make sure the main message you want to convey is as obvious as possible. Insert it early in the content, and repeat it at strategic points throughout. Again, your audience should never have to struggle to figure out what the point of your content is or what you're trying to say.

Not every one of these pointers applies to every piece of content. But in general, the main goal of advocates during content development should be to convey a clear message that is relevant to their target audience. Do that, and your content will succeed in advancing the goals of advocacy.

Review

Before publishing content, it's ideal to have advocates or other stakeholders within a community review it. The purpose of review is to find faults that may undercut the content's value.

The main type of problem that arises during review is technical accuracy. If content gets technical details wrong, it loses its credibility in the eyes of developers. By having technically skilled people other than the content author review content, technical mistakes or oversights can be caught.

Importantly, reviews shouldn't be a time to question the opinions behind content. As long as the idea driving a piece is technically sound, the content should be considered solid. There may be alternative ways of doing something, and in some cases, advocates may find that internal stakeholders in a business fundamentally question their technical views. But the point of advocacy work is not to achieve internal consensus about messaging and push that messaging relentlessly. It's to engage technical audiences, and sometimes, differences of opinion are necessary for that purpose. After all, developers likely have differing opinions about various topics, so advocates may need to have different opinions to engage with them effectively.

It's important, too, to avoid review processes that are too long or complex. As a rule, each piece of content should be reviewed by no more than three people; more than that and you're likely to run into review cycles that take too long and result in too much feedback to be usable. The main purpose of the review process is to ensure that content meets basic standards for technical accuracy, not to spend hours debating every sentence in a piece.

To put all of this another way: Reviews shouldn't focus on trying to make content "perfect" because perfection doesn't exist. Content is always subjective, and too many suggestions for changes to content slow down publication cycles without adding real value. Instead, the goal of review should be to ensure that content meets basic technical accuracy standards. As long as it does, it should move to publication.

Publication

Publication is often the hardest part of content operations for advocates, mainly because it's not always obvious where to publish pieces.

Media channels owned by the advocates' business – such as company blogs or video channels – are one obvious place for publication. However, content published in these locations may not reach broad audiences because developers are less likely, in general, to follow company-owned media than they are to consume general-purpose media.

For that reason, it's wise for advocates in many cases to build relationships with third-party media sites and publish content on them occasionally. Most sites are happy to have the content as long as it's not explicitly promotional of a company's brand or tools.

Partners' and customers' channels are another option to consider for publishing content. These channels tend to be subject to the same readership limitations as a company's own channels, but there is added value in having content appear on a site owned by someone else, even if it's another vendor. The content appears more credible, and the publishing relationship can help to strengthen ties with partners or customers.

Keep in mind, too, that there is no reason in many cases why advocates can't cross-publish content across multiple channels. Content published on a third-party site could also be published on a company's own site. Just remember to include links between each instance of the content so it doesn't appear that you're trying to double-post without acknowledging that the content exists elsewhere.

Measurement

Measuring the impact of content may seem easy, especially for stakeholders who think in terms of basic metrics like how many times a piece was read or viewed. The reality, however, is that simple metrics don't reliably reflect content's overall impact.

For example, a blog post might achieve a large number of views simply because it's published on a major media site. But if few developers inside a target community read that site, the blog is unlikely to be very successful in advancing the goals of advocates. It would be better for the blog to be read just a few hundred times through a link shared on a Slack channel used by the target developers than to be read ten thousand times through a popular media site where fewer than 1 percent of readers are from the advocates' target audience.

Another, slightly more sophisticated way of trying to measure content's impact is to track how many actions the audience takes based on the content. For example, you could include a "call to action" link inviting readers of a blog post to sign up for a newsletter. This is better than counting very crude metrics like total reads, but it's not an excellent way of measuring impact because it doesn't directly measure how much readers actually engaged with the content. Not all readers who engaged with the content or were impacted by it will sign up for the newsletter, and not all people who sign up for the newsletter will have used the content in a meaningful way.

A better approach is to monitor metrics that do reflect direct engagement. For example, advocates could include code within an article that pulls data from a server or repository where they can track how many times the data was downloaded. By measuring data downloads, they can track how many people actually ran the commands inside the article. That's a much more meaningful measure of engagement than simply looking at how many people opened the article or clicked a link at the end. Not everyone who reads and is impacted by the article will have run the commands, of course, but there's nonetheless likely to be a better correlation between engagement and the commands than between engagement and newsletter signups.

More broadly, advocates can measure content's impact by assessing how higher-level actions coordinate with content messaging. For example, if advocates produce a series of content focused on a new technical feature in their company's product, they could then measure how many developers in their community begin using the feature in the months following the content's publication. Although not all feature uptake can be attributed to the content, there is a general correlation here that can be measured.

If it sounds like we're suggesting that advocates and businesses should not be overly obsessed with granular precision when it comes to measuring content's impact, it's because we are. Bean counting may feel satisfying, but it rarely helps organizations make effective decisions about which content drives meaningful engagement and which doesn't. It's better to err on the side of blunt measures that provide an overall – if imperfect – sense of actual engagement than to count laser-focused metrics that are easy to track but that don't necessarily align closely with engagement.

Other Notes on Content Strategy

We've described what it takes to curate, develop, review, publish, and measure effective content. Let us add a few pointers that should also guide content strategies for advocates, at all steps of the process.

Boring Content Can Be Good Content

Advocates might naturally aspire to write content that is exciting. The reality, though, is that – although exciting content has its place – a lot of the content that advocates produce will feel boring, in the sense that it deals with relatively dense technical topics that no one gets fired up about.

That sort of content is necessary because not every topic developer audiences care about is flashy or thought-provoking. Sometimes, developers just want a tutorial on how to use a product feature or how to write an API call, for example. If the content meets a developer need, it drives engagement, so it's successful – even if it's not electrifying or alluring.

Spell Out Prerequisites

Often, certain types of technical content – especially tutorials – require readers or viewers to perform certain prerequisite steps before they can follow along. They might need to have certain tools installed on their systems, for example, or have specific configurations in place.

Advocates should be sure to spell out prerequisites like these clearly and never to over-assume that their audience has the same environment or experience they do. Although how-to articles might not spell out exactly how to meet prerequisites, they should outline the process or link to other explanatory resources wherever possible.

You don't want your content to turn your audience off because it asks them to do things they can't do for lack of prerequisites.

On Viral Content

Producing content that goes viral – meaning it receives massive views in a short period and/or is widely shared through channels like social media – may be the dream of content marketers around the world. But again, advocates aren't marketers, and viral content shouldn't be the goal of advocacy content operations. On the contrary, attempting to produce viral content can be a major distraction for advocates.

Part of the reason why is that no one can predict what makes for viral content. There's no formula you can follow to ensure that your articles or videos will reach hundreds of thousands of users in the first day after publication. Instead, virality boils down mostly to luck, so spending time trying to curate and develop content that will go viral is a fool's errand.

The second problem with chasing the viral content dream is that viral content is not necessarily effective content for the purpose of advocacy. Just because a large number of people read a blog post doesn't mean they meaningfully engage with it. And while viral content may help to build awareness of a company's brand – or raise the profile of the advocate who authored it – those actions are not the primary goal of advocacy. Advocacy is instead about engaging meaningfully with developer audiences, which involves more than building name recognition.

SEO and Advocacy Content

Another way to waste time when developing content for advocacy purposes is to obsess over Search Engine Optimization, or SEO.

It's useful to take basic steps to make content friendly toward search engines – such as including relevant keywords in headers. To that end, advocates who create content published on the Web should be familiar with the most basic best practices that help to ensure their content is organized and labeled in ways that search engines expect.

However, spending too much time on SEO is not valuable in most cases. Just as no one can guarantee that content will go viral, no one can guarantee that specific SEO practices will result in a first-place ranking, because search engine algorithms are black boxes that no one fully understands. So trying to optimize every aspect of your content for SEO is a waste of time.

Plus, even if your content is in the top place, it may not matter much for advocacy purposes. Developers won't care much about content that looks good to search engines but lacks the technical relevance or depth that developers care about.

The bottom line: While SEO deserves a little thought in the content development process, it should never become a priority that distracts from what really matters to developer audiences, which is high-quality, accurate, impactful technical information.

Content Series

It can be tempting to plan to publish content using a series. For example, advocates might develop multiple blog posts that they release a week apart, with each post building on an idea from a previous post.

In a perfect world, developer audiences would follow such series closely, excitedly anticipating each new installment. But in the real world, developers probably are not paying that much attention to your content channels, so the series strategy doesn't actually build anticipation. Instead, it leaves you with content items that are incomplete when consumed individually. It forces content consumers to navigate between multiple individual pieces in order to follow a discussion that runs throughout multiple pieces, which can be frustrating.

For these reasons, content series violate the advice we gave previously that simpler content is better content and that content consumers should never have to try hard to understand what your content is about or how to use it. As a rule, we recommend avoiding content series. Instead, create content that is self-contained, meaning each item that you publish can be consumed independently.

Gated Content

Content marketers love to "gate" content. Gating means placing content behind a registration page that requires users to share contact information in order to access content.

This makes sense from the perspective of marketing, where generating leads and ensuring that marketers can reach them is a primary goal. But it doesn't often help advocates. There is rarely a reason for advocates to collect names, email addresses, and other personal information from the developers they are trying to reach. And doing so can harm advocacy efforts because it leaves developers feeling like the advocate is more interested in selling to them than in engaging with them in meaningful technical conversations. It will also result in many potential readers choosing not to view content at all because they don't want to register.

So, avoid gating content that is targeted at developer audiences, unless you truly have a good reason to gate it. It's better to make the content as easy to access as possible in order to increase authenticity and engagement. Generating leads should be the job of marketers and marketing content, not advocates and advocacy content.

Conclusion

Content is arguably the single most important tool for engaging developer audiences efficiently and at scale, but it's also one of the most complicated tools to leverage. Deciding which topics to focus on, which types of content to create, and where to publish requires a deep understanding of audience needs. Creating good content also requires excellent skills in a variety of areas, and there are many pitfalls that advocates can run into along the way – like spending too much time on SEO initiatives or having unrealistic expectations about the virality of one's content. Avoid these issues and focus on qualities that drive successful content to lay a healthy foundation for your advocacy program.

Understanding and Optimizing Stakeholders in Developer Advocacy

We've mentioned "stakeholders" a number of times so far in this book in reference to people who collaborate with or require support from developer advocates. But we haven't really defined in any systematic way who those stakeholders are or exactly how they should interface with advocates.

C. Riley and C. Tozzi, *Developer Advocacy*,
https://doi.org/10.1007/978-1-4842-9597-7_6

We saved that discussion for this chapter, which dives into how stakeholders across the business can help to start and support a developer advocacy program. By stakeholders, we mean various types of people inside a business who are not developer advocates themselves but who play important roles in guiding, supporting, or otherwise engaging with advocates.

Stakeholder Engagement As the Key to Cross-Functional Collaboration

Collaboration with stakeholders is a critical topic because advocacy is inherently cross-functional. Although organizations that invest in developer advocacy typically have a stand-alone team of developer advocates, those advocates must constantly interface with other stakeholders to do their jobs well. They must work with product managers and sales and marketing teams to help drive content operations, for example. They may require technical information from the business's software developers, which they can in turn share with external developer communities as part of guidance or thought leadership initiatives. Even more so than business functions like sales and marketing – which also require a fair amount of collaboration and coordination with other parts of the organization – advocacy doesn't work well at all without an efficient and scalable way of engaging with people in other roles.

By the way, it's not just for the sake of internal advocacy that advocates must work with other stakeholders. That's part of the reason; advocates can't represent external developer communities to other members of the business very well if they lack an efficient means of connecting to those members. But at the same time, effective external advocacy requires close collaboration between advocates and internal business stakeholders, because it's only through that collaboration that advocates know what's happening in the business and, by extension, can tailor their engagement with external developer communities to reflect internal business goals, priorities, and direction – such as which product features the company is working on or which use cases or market needs it's targeting.

> It is important to have different altitudes of a strategy from bite size which can be shared widely to a deeper dive. I have seen most people only have the deep explanation. Sometimes when communicating a strategy you only have 5 mins, and now that most companies are hybrid information is shared multi-channel. You need to consider all of this. However, the measurement and KPIs you are chasing I have found are always critical. Once you have a crips strategy, share by radiating outwards from your team, to your core stakeholders, to the broader organization.

—Sara Rosso, Technical Marketing Leader

Stakeholders in Advocacy Operations

Now that we've explained why collaboration with various stakeholders inside the business is so important for successful developer advocacy, let's look at precisely who those stakeholders are and how they ideally interface with advocates.

Developer Marketers

While not all businesses have developer marketing functions, those that do employ marketers who focus on developer audiences are an obvious stakeholder in developer advocacy operations. It's important not to conflate developer advocacy with developer marketing; both are separate roles because the primary purpose of developer marketers is to communicate the value of products and services, whereas advocates have a broader, less economics-driven mission focused on engagement and relationship building. Nonetheless, developer marketers can provide support to advocates in a number of ways, and vice versa.

For one, developer marketers can deliver high-level messaging that guides the efforts of advocates. In turn, advocates can provide feedback on the messaging that marketers pursue. Since advocates know the personas and technical needs of developer communities better than anyone else inside the business, they can offer uniquely valuable feedback about messaging. That said, at the end of the day, curating marketing messaging is the responsibility of marketers, so the marketing team should own final decision-making in this vein.

Another valuable way for advocates to interface with developer marketers is to collaborate on content initiatives. As we explained in the previous chapter, the content that advocates create should be different from generic marketing content, but that doesn't mean that advocates and marketers can't work together to share insights about which types of content and topics will best speak to developer audiences. Both groups may have different perspectives on the content needs of the developers they are seeking to engage, and rather than working in isolation on content, they should work to support and reinforce each other.

Along similar lines, because advocates typically have a technical depth that marketers lack, advocates may be able to assist in developing technical aspects of marketing content – or sharing parts of advocacy content that marketers import into their own content. Once again, it's important to emphasize that advocates shouldn't be turned into mere content writers for the marketing team, but the marketing team can benefit from the unique technical skills that advocates possess when working on content – just as advocates can benefit from the unique messaging skills and strategies of marketers, even though those messages shouldn't be at the center of advocacy content.

Engineering

Engineering teams are another key stakeholder in developer advocacy. In any business that develops technical products, advocates must work closely with engineers to understand the product and its implementation. Advocates should know what's coming next in the feature pipeline. They should also understand intended use cases and deployment techniques for products so that they can share best-practices guidance with external developers.

At the same time, as we've noted in earlier chapters, advocates can support engineering teams by offering advice on product or feature implementation. Most engineers don't directly interface with external developers who use the products they build, but advocates do, so advocates are in a unique position to offer technical feedback to engineering teams as products are being built. There are other ways of collecting feedback, such as surveying external developers after a product or new feature has appeared, but by working with advocates during the design and implementation process, engineers leverage the benefit of being able to integrate the perspectives and needs of external developers into products early on, rather than waiting until after release to discover and correct issues that negatively impact the external developer experience.

Advocates' engagement with external developers, combined with their technical expertise, also positions them to advise the engineering team on fixing bugs or unexpected behavior within technical products. Although tasks like debugging, troubleshooting, and end-user support should never be a primary responsibility of advocates, advocates can help to guide other stakeholders as they work through those issues, ensuring that external developer needs and perspectives are represented throughout the process.

Product Management

Product management teams are among the groups that stand to gain the most from engagement with developer advocates. At the same time, however, the relationship between advocates and product managers can be one of the most tenuous.

The main reason why is that product management teams have a tendency to assume that they have unique insights into what external developers need. After all, understanding audience needs and translating that insight into product enhancements is one of the chief responsibilities of product managers, so if product managers appear not to have as strong of a command of external developer desires as advocates, they may fear that they will lose value in the eyes of the business.

To address this challenge and avoid turning the advocacy-product management relationship into one of conflict and competition (with each group vying to prove that it "gets" external developers better than the other), businesses should encourage each group to contribute different types of perspective on external developer needs. In most cases, product managers devote their efforts to specific products, or even specific ranges of functionality within a single product. They don't own or manage a business's entire suite of products. In contrast, developer advocates do typically engage with external communities based on a broad set of products. As a result, advocates are more holistic in their understanding of how external developers use and experience products.

What this means is that product managers are in the best position to generate insight about what external developers need from a specific feature or product, whereas advocates can best advise on how an individual feature or product might fit within the external developer experience as a whole. To put this another way, product managers might know how adding a new feature could enhance the way developers use a particular product, but advocates are in a better position to say whether adding the feature might attract developers away from other of the company's products and to the new one, or how the new feature could complement other products that the business offers.

In addition, advocates can offer special perspective to product managers because the feedback that advocates collect from developer communities is less likely to be tainted by an understanding that product developers have specific goals in mind – goals usually associated with maximizing product adoption and engagement. In contrast, advocates are more likely to be seen as people who seek genuine engagement with external developer communities and, by that token, to collect purer feedback from developer communities. Developers might tell product managers what they think they want to hear to drive tool adoption, in other words, whereas developers are more likely to tell advocates how they actually use a product and what they value most in it.

Along similar lines, whereas product managers are more likely to have relationships with developers who already use a company's products – especially paying users – advocates are in a stronger position to engage with developers who represent a broader segment of the external developer community. That means they can deliver insights to guide product development that product managers might miss if they perform research based on the needs and usage patterns of developers who have already bought into a company's offerings, overlooking developers who are active in the ecosystem but are not yet key users.

Beyond collaborating on product development, advocates can work with product managers to gain insights that help support advocacy operations. Product managers should keep advocates informed of what's coming next on the product road map, for example. They can also share information about how they *expect* external developers to use new features so that advocates can then validate through their engagement with external communities whether actual usage aligns with those expectations.

For their part, advocates can support product managers in ways that extend beyond feature planning and assessment. They can help create technical content to support feature launches, for example, or help make new features available to beta users within external developer communities prior to general launch.

In short, product management teams and developer advocates should work closely together in ways that allow each group to leverage its unique strengths and capabilities in the context of product planning and development. When both groups collaborate rather than compete, the business benefits through smoother product management operations and by delivering features that better meet the needs and expectations of external developers.

Developer Relations

For larger organizations, and in organizations where engaging with external developers is a central business priority, a unit dedicated to developer relationships may exist. If this is the case, developer advocates typically work as part of this group. But they are only one part of the developer relations team, and they must interface with other stakeholders within that group.

Developer relations teams can be organized in many ways, so the exact structure and nature of collaboration between developer advocates and other developer relations stakeholders will vary. In general, however, advocates should expect to interface with other developer relations stakeholders who are responsible for functions like planning programs and events for external developer communities, producing documentation targeted at external developers, and ecosystem management (which involves managing relationships with developers at partner businesses within an organization's ecosystem).

Here's a breakdown of how advocates can engage with other members of the developer relations team working in these areas.

Programs and Events

The programs and events teams are responsible for organizing campaigns that bring developers together. These initiatives represent a combination of developer experience from a content perspective and marketing from a promotional and event perspective. Among other purposes, these events give advocates a platform for sharing content.

Advocates can support programs and events teams with content planning. For example, advocates might help recruit and vet speakers at developer conferences, or even plan event themes. Advocates can also be speakers themselves, which is one example of how they can provide content during events.

Documentation

Although advocates shouldn't generally be tasked with writing documentation, advocacy should provide documentation teams with advice about how best to organize and publish content in ways that serve external developer needs. Advocates can also make suggestions about technical details that are missing from documentation but that might benefit external developers, and they can recommend examples or use cases to detail inside documentation that align with developer needs.

On top of this, the content that advocates develop can serve to complement or augment documentation. For example, product tutorials or demos could be integrated into documentation to add context or examples that guide external developers as they peruse documentation.

Ecosystem Management

For businesses that need to manage relationships not just with external developer communities in general but also with developers at partner businesses, advocates can work closely to address technical issues, provide guidance on architecture and best practices, and share content.

These activities are important because the goal of ecosystem management – a function commonly seen at SaaS companies – is to ensure that partner networks are able to consume a business's technical products and APIs effectively. These partnerships tend to have a more strategic focus than product usage by generic third-party developers, which makes engaging effectively with developers are partner organizations especially critical.

Beyond the Obvious: Other Forms of Stakeholder Engagement

The stakeholder types and engagement activities we've described previously certainly don't represent all of the potential ways in which advocates can work with other stakeholders inside the business. We've focused only on the most obvious and important stakeholders for engagement at the typical organization.

Advocates might also work closely with sales and marketing teams, for example, to whom they can provide guidance on how best to engage with technical audiences. Since advocates specialize in understanding the needs of developers and translating them into language that nontechnical stakeholders can understand, advocates can offer sales and marketing advice that is difficult to obtain by other means.

Similarly, customer relations teams can benefit from advocates as a source of guidance and advice not just about troubleshooting technical issues but also about understanding how to prioritize competing customer needs, at least in cases where those customers are external developers.

These are just some examples of how advocates can engage cross-functionality across the business. Ultimately, what matters most for ensuring successful stakeholder engagement is for business leaders, and advocates themselves, to recognize that advocacy is an inherently flexible and cross-functional domain. Advocates should never be forced into one silo within the business or required to interface with other stakeholders in rigidly structured ways.

Instead, to get the most from advocacy, treat advocates as a resource that can be leveraged in a multitude of ways to guide, inform, and support other parts of the business. Be sure, too, to focus on opportunities that draw on the unique perspectives of advocates. There may be some overlap between advocates and other stakeholders, and rather than using advocates in redundant ways – and in ways that may put them in conflict with other stakeholders who are trying to do the same things – advocates are best leveraged to provide unique value that other business functions can't deliver.

Growing: Creating an Advocacy Road Map

So far in this book, we've covered why and how to get started with a developer advocacy function in your business. But starting developer advocacy is, of course, only the first step in leveraging advocacy to help drive business success. To reap a return on your investment in advocacy operations and ensure that your business benefits from advocacy over the long term, you need a plan for growing and sustaining the advocacy program over time.

The best way to do this is to establish a road map that lays out how your advocacy initiative will grow over time. A road map ensures that you avoid ad hoc decision-making about shaping the evolution of the advocacy program. It also allows you to be proactive about meeting challenges like changes in advocacy personnel – which, if not handled properly, could stunt the growth of effective advocacy.

© Chris Riley, Chris Tozzi 2023
C. Riley and C. Tozzi, *Developer Advocacy*,
https://doi.org/10.1007/978-1-4842-9597-7_7

This chapter walks through the process of creating an advocacy road map. It also explains how businesses should expect advocacy programs to grow over time, and it highlights some of the key challenges that tend to arise along the way as advocacy operations scale up.

What is an Advocacy Road Map?

An advocacy road map is a formal plan that describes how a business's developer advocacy program will grow over time. It addresses details such as

- How rapidly the business adds new advocates to its team in order to increase overall team size

- How the advocacy program will react if a key advocate departs for another job

- Strategies for training and mentoring new advocates

- Approaches to measuring the effectiveness of advocacy operations in order to secure buy-in for advocacy team growth

- Conditions that determine when the advocacy team is "big enough" and no longer needs to keep growing

In addition to these considerations, which apply to virtually any advocacy program, your business may choose to factor other priorities into its advocacy road map that reflect its unique requirements. For example, if the business acquires other companies on a regular basis, the way that the advocacy team reacts to acquisition events (which could have wide-ranging implications for the nature and scale of advocacy operations, especially if the business that gets acquired has products or services that engage external developers) should factor into the road map.

The Importance of an Advocacy Road Map

Again, having an advocacy road map is important because it allows advocacy teams and business stakeholders to address growth-related challenges proactively and with foresight, rather than having to react in the moment to unexpected challenges or inventing advocacy growth strategies as they go along. Like the playbooks that IT engineers use to guide incident response operations or the product road maps that developers and product management teams rely on to shape the implementation of new features, an advocacy road map establishes a formal, comprehensive plan to guide advocacy program growth.

In addition, advocacy road maps help ensure that advocacy programs can make the difficult leap from operating on a very small scale to growing into an operation that is large enough to benefit the business as a whole. As we mentioned in earlier chapters, it's common for advocacy teams to originate with just a single advocate – which is appropriate for small companies that are just launching products, or for businesses where senior management has not yet fully bought into the idea of investing in advocacy. But a very small advocacy team is insufficient for enterprise-scale operations, so it's critical to have a growth plan in place in order to leverage the full potential of advocacy.

On top of that, very small advocacy teams are at risk of being upended or having to reinvent their operational strategy every time a change in personnel occurs. If you have just a single advocate on staff, that person's departure for a new job could disrupt your advocacy operations for months, or (in extreme cases) lead to the abandonment of the business's advocacy program entirely. And with just a few advocates on hand, departures could lead to dramatic diminishment of advocacy operations and engagement, which negatively impacts external developers' view of the brand and product.

The bottom line here is that it's a major mistake to leave advocacy team growth to chance, or to assume that your advocates will figure out how to work through growing pains on their own. Instead, you need a plan that spells out how to grow this important but complex function within the business.

Shaping the Road Map: The Seven Maturity Stages of Advocacy Growth

As we noted earlier, the exact components of an advocacy road map may vary depending on business needs and priorities. So, rather than thinking in terms of specific elements to include in a road map, it's helpful to shape your road map in terms of the maturity stages that it needs to support. By this, we mean that your road map should be designed to allow your advocacy program to meet specific milestones that align with the overall maturity and sophistication of your advocacy operations.

There are seven key maturity stages that businesses should target.

Stage 1: Brute-Force Engagement

An advocacy team is least mature when it's new and small. At this stage, it's common to take what we call a brute-force approach to engagement operations, which means that your advocates (or advocate, in the likely event that you have just one) focus on high-impact, nonsystematic engagement with external developers. Rather than operating according to a complex plan and having detailed processes in place, the advocacy team meets developers where and when it can, striving to achieve maximal impact with limited personnel resources.

Given the low level of structure and sophistication of this stage, your advocacy road map doesn't need to address special issues or challenges to support this level of maturity. This is where road maps start by default.

Stage 2: Scaling Beyond Individuals

A slightly more mature advocacy team is one that leverages tools and processes to scale its operations in such a way that total engagement with external developers is not dependent solely on the number of advocates on the team. The following chapter discusses this topic in more detail, but as a basic example of amplifying impact, advocates might leverage content that can be republished across multiple channels to amplify the scale of engagement.

Overall, engagement is limited at this stage; it is not systematic or comprehensive enough to unlock the full potential of advocacy for the business as a whole. But there is more maturity than under a brute-force model that is tied entirely to the presence and initiative of individual advocates.

To achieve this stage of maturity, your road map needs to establish the processes and resources that advocates will use to scale engagement operations. Those components can vary depending on which scalability strategy advocates choose. But again, they might include resources like content, which is one way to scale the impact of advocacy beyond direct and personal engagement by individual advocates.

Stage 3: Adding Internal Advocacy

The third stage of maturity is the one where the advocacy team expands its focus to include internal advocacy, not just engagement with external developers. This often requires increasing the size of the advocacy team, so your road map should include goals for the total number of advocates necessary to support internal and external advocacy operations simultaneously.

In addition, the road map should spell out where internal advocacy operations will start. It's often not realistic to engage with every internal stakeholder from the beginning, so the road map should identify which stakeholders (such as the marketing team or the product management team) are the highest priority for early-stage internal advocacy operations.

Stage 4: Systematizing Advocacy

Once advocacy is taking place both externally and internally, and the size of the advocacy team is large enough to support both facets of engagement, the advocacy team is in a position to systematize its operations. This means formally spelling out what advocates do and how they do it. When the team reaches this level of maturity, it becomes much more resilient against challenges like changes in personnel, because it's no longer dependent on the initiative of individual advocates; instead, it has a process-centered operational approach that can be embraced by any qualified personnel.

To enable this stage, the road map should detail how the business will supply the resources that advocates need to operate in a systematic way, such as tools and funding to support full-scale content operations and regular advocate travel to relevant events.

Step 5: Scale Internal Advocacy

After establishing a formal and systematic approach to advocacy, the advocacy program is ready to scale up internal advocacy operations. As we mentioned, internal advocacy efforts may be limited at first, but as the advocacy program matures, internal advocacy should expand to all stakeholders.

The main road map requirement for this maturity stage is more personnel in order to support full-scale internal advocacy without compromising on external advocacy.

Step 6: Achieving "Flow"

As the advocacy program nears full maturity, it should be able to achieve what might be called a flow state. This means that advocates have become an embedded resource within the standard flow of all relevant business functions – sales, marketing, product development, and beyond. In other words, rather than serving as a special resource that the business leverages only in certain situations, advocacy is an intrinsic part of all operations where it can provide value. No one has to think about including the advocates in key business processes and decisions because the advocates are embedded within these functions by default.

This level of maturity doesn't require the allocation of specific resources as much as it requires ensuring full awareness of and buy-in for advocacy from across the business. Thus, the road map should detail how advocates will ensure that their value is fully recognized – which data they need to collect to demonstrate value, how they communicate the value to stakeholders, and so on.

Step 7: Continuous Realignment

The final stage of maturity is one where the advocacy team is able to react constantly and seamlessly to new challenges and business needs as they arise. Business requirements are always evolving, which means that the best ways that advocates can support the business will also change. New product features may require engagement with new external developer communities, for example, or restructuring inside the business may change the way advocates interface with internal stakeholders. The most mature advocacy teams can respond to changes like this with aplomb because they are adept at interpreting business needs and changing their processes to suit them.

As with the "flow" stage of maturity, this stage doesn't require additional resources or personnel as much as it requires the establishment of processes that ensure that advocates have visibility into business needs, as well as the freedom to react to those needs. In some cases, this stage may require loosening the rigidity of processes established in earlier stages so that advocates are not constrained by narrowly defined operational rules. Once your team is fully mature and has fully scaled both external and internal advocacy, it should receive the trust and freedom to operate according to its best judgment.

Growing the Team

As we noted in the preceding section, increasing the maturity of advocacy operations doesn't necessarily require growing your developer team in many cases. For that reason, it's important to decouple team growth from the advocacy road map. The road map should identify points where team growth is necessary, but increasing advocacy headcount and growing advocacy operations are different endeavors that require different plans.

With that reality in mind, let's explore what it does look like to grow an advocacy team. Here again, the process can be broken down into distinct stages.

Stage 1: Hiring Your First Advocates

When you're just starting an advocacy function, your priority in creating the team should be on hiring advocates who already have an established profile in external developer communities and a record of engagement. These individuals are often hard to identify, but as we mentioned in previous chapters, you might find candidates who already exist inside your organization in other roles (like engineering or sales) and who can become the first official advocates for your business.

Alternatively, look for members of external developer communities who have already established close ties to your business and demonstrated enthusiasm for its products. If they are also adept at communication and understanding the principles of advocacy, they may also help you start your advocacy team.

Stage 2: Stabilize the Team

It can be tempting, after hiring your first few advocates, to seek to grow the team rapidly. But a better approach is to invest in stabilizing the talent you already have on your advocacy team and amplify the impact of their work. Ensure that your existing advocates understand what their mission is and which value they bring to the business, and celebrate their early successes in driving engagement.

There are two reasons to prioritize team stabilization over team growth early on. One is that if you grow advocacy headcount before you've systematized advocacy operations, you may end up with too many advocates and too little structure to ensure that they are not doing redundant work or stepping on each other's toes.

The second reason is that good advocates are difficult to hire and retain, and so from a practical and strategic perspective, it's easier in many cases to keep the advocates you already have – and who already know your product and have an established presence within your target developer communities – than to try to hire additional ones.

Stage 3: Broaden Team Structure

After you have stabilized your nascent advocacy team, you're in a position to begin growing it slowly by hiring additional advocates. However, the focus at this point should be less on scaling up the advocacy program and more on establishing a career ladder so that your current advocates have room to grow.

So, as your existing advocates prove their value and achieve wins, promote them and hire additional advocates to fill lower-level advocacy roles. This approach allows your advocacy team to grow with purpose and in a way that intrinsically rewards advocates for positive contributions, as opposed to simply growing for the relatively arbitrary goal of increasing total headcount.

Stage 4: Scale for Product Coverage

With a career ladder in place for your advocates, your next step in team growth should be on broadening product coverage. With smaller advocacy teams, advocates can typically only support certain products or product features, and they can sustain limited scopes of engagement with external and internal stakeholders. But as your team grows, aim to hit a point where all products and all communities are supported.

At this stage, it becomes less important to hire advocates based on their community profiles and more important to ensure they have product expertise. In other words, whereas early on you should look for individuals who are already operating as advocates (even though they may not think of themselves as such), once you have an established and mature team, you can begin hiring people who don't necessarily have advocacy experience but who have product expertise and can be trained to work as advocates.

Stage 5: Sustain the Team

With a team in place that covers full product functionality, the next major growth stage is to ensure that the team is set up for long-term success. You may not need to hire more advocates at this stage, but you might hire a program manager or operations manager who can help to support advocates and coordinate their activities. Creating mentorship programs for the advocacy team is also a wise investment because it helps advocates achieve visibility into each other's operations and share best practices.

Stage 6: Establish Senior Leadership

Although you should establish career ladders for advocates earlier in the growth process, it's not until your team is mature and operating at full scale that you should bring in a senior advocate leader or director. Many advocacy programs operate for years before they reach this stage.

The purpose of a senior advocate leader is not just to oversee the advocacy team but to serve in a cross-functional role that helps to align advocacy efforts with business priorities. The leader should have advocacy experience but should not operate as an advocate on a day-to-day basis; instead, the focus should be on cultivating strategy and helping to achieve the continuous realignment maturity stage described earlier in this chapter.

Stage 7: Gap-Based Growth

Of course, simply having a senior advocacy leader is not enough to ensure continuous alignment between advocacy and business goals. You should also be prepared to react to emerging challenges by making additional hires based on quantifiable gaps within your advocacy program.

For example, by collecting metrics about the portion of relevant external developers whom your advocates are reaching, you can identify when advocates who focus on certain communities have become overstretched and there is a need to hire new ones. The launch of new products of product features is also an example of an event that may require additional advocacy team growth.

The point here is that you should establish processes that allow you to identify when additional advocates are needed – either for reasons of overall scale or due to new product coverage requirements – and use that information to guide additional hiring.

Conclusion

The advocacy function, and the personnel who drive it, would be easy to manage if it included just a handful of people and limited reach. But leveraging the complete potential of advocacy requires the ability to grow advocacy teams and operations over time. The total size of advocacy teams may vary depending on many factors (such as how large your business is and how many external developers and individual products it needs to support), but virtually every company must have a growth plan in place that systematically spells out how the team will scale up over time and which maturity milestones it will focus on achieving as it grows.

This chapter addressed the fundamentals of the scaling process by detailing how to establish a road map and how to plan for team growth. In the next two chapters, we'll dive deeper into other dimensions of advocacy growth, starting with how to amplify success so that the impact of advocacy operations is not closely tied to the total number of advocates but is shaped instead by how the advocates work and where they focus their efforts.

Amplifying Advocacy's Impact

The previous chapter laid out why and how to establish a road map in order to drive the growth of the developer advocacy function. It also discussed topics like how to grow the size of the advocacy team over time and which milestones advocates should work toward as they grow.

What Chapter 7 didn't address in detail, however, is how to amplify the impact of individual advocates. That topic is sufficiently complex to require a chapter of its own – this one. In the following pages, we will explain specific strategies and practices that can maximize the impact of every advocate on your team in the context of both internal and external advocacy efforts. The goal of these tips is to highlight ways in which advocacy organizations can maximize their value and optimize the relationship between advocates and the business.

© Chris Riley, Chris Tozzi 2023
C. Riley and C. Tozzi, *Developer Advocacy*,
https://doi.org/10.1007/978-1-4842-9597-7_8

Going Beyond the Body Shop

Before diving into strategies for maximizing the impact of advocates, let's first go over why doing so is a worthwhile endeavor.

The main reason is that, as we have said before and will say again before the book is over, most advocacy teams are relatively small — as small as just a single advocate. Yet the operations and business needs that those teams must support tend to be quite large.

As a result, maximizing the impact of individual advocates — which means increasing their reach among both external and internal communities, as well as helping them to operate efficiently and with minimal business resources — is the only practical way to ensure that advocates can meet the business's needs effectively.

We say this is the "only practical way" because you could, of course, focus on simply increasing your advocacy team's size in order to scale up their impact. But that leaves you in the position of running a "body shop." You can't scale efforts unless you hire new advocates, and depending on the experience and influence that the advocate brings with them, the impact of adding an advocate might not achieve what you hoped.

On top of this, there is the challenge that skilled advocates are few and far between. Few people specialize in advocacy compared to other roles. And even if you draw on internal talent you have within other business units, as we suggested in earlier chapters, to identify individuals who could succeed as advocates, you will almost certainly find that there is a very small pool of people to devote to advocacy efforts.

So, instead of treating advocacy scaling as a matter merely of increasing overall team size, it's important to look for other ways to scale up impact without necessarily scaling up headcount.

To be clear, we're not suggesting that growing the size of the team is not important. At the end of the day, large-scale, long-term advocacy operations require a sizable team, so business stakeholders should be on the lookout for opportunities to add talented advocates to their organization. But they shouldn't treat headcount increase as the only, or the primary, means of scaling up advocacy impact or effort.

Scaling Methodologies

Now that we know why scaling advocacy's impact without necessarily scaling advocate headcount is important, let's look at specific strategies for achieving this goal.

Advocate-to-Advocate Data Sharing and Collaboration

The single most effective strategy that advocacy teams can embrace to amplify their impact is to share and collaborate among one another.

Now, this may seem obvious. Most teams recognize the value of sharing between team members, of course.

But when it comes to advocacy, the importance of sharing and collaboration can be easy to overlook, simply because of the way advocates operate. By its nature, advocacy is more of an individualistic endeavor than many other business functions, such as marketing or engineering. Few individual marketers would create a campaign in total isolation from the rest of their team, just as virtually no engineer would develop an application or troubleshoot a system without coordinating with other engineers.

But when it comes to advocacy, because each advocate tends to engage with a different community and bring different skills and viewpoints to the table, advocacy teams face a higher risk of becoming siloed, or even having each advocate operate as if they are a team of one when that's not actually the case.

To avoid this risk, it's critical for advocates to share information, resources, and workflows wherever possible. Actionable methods for doing so include the following:

- Maintaining wikis that document advocacy resources and that advocates can easily update over time.

- Developing internal podcasts or newsletters where advocates discuss advocacy work. In addition to keeping other advocates informed of their efforts, these resources can advance the goal of helping the rest of the business understand what advocates do and which services they offer to internal stakeholders.

- Creating an onboarding system where new advocates can ask questions and where answers are reported. This is another resource that can help advocates understand what other advocates in the organization are doing and streamline their operations.

The list could go on, but the point is: wherever possible, advocates should document what they are doing and share the information with other advocates. Ideally, such information will always come in written form so that it can be easily maintained and handed off to others. The more resource sharing and collaboration that take place between advocates, the higher the overall impact of the advocacy team will be.

Shared Budgets

Another way to increase collaboration between advocates is to establish shared budgets for specific types of advocacy work. Shared budgets mean that the team as a whole receives a financial allocation to support a given effort, such as content development and distribution, rather than awarding funds on an advocate-by-advocate basis.

Shared budgeting fosters collaboration because it encourages – and, in some cases, even requires – advocates to work together. When an advocate can't spend money unless other advocates are on board, the result typically is less redundancy and more collaboration.

As an example of what shared budgeting might look like in practice, imagine an advocacy team that receives a collective budget for publishing paid content. The need to share in the funds means that each advocate must be aware of which paid content other advocates are developing and how best to create new content that complements rather than reiterates other advocates' work. As a result, the overall paid content operations of the team are likely to be more impactful, not to mention more efficient, both of which translate to increased advocacy value for the business without an increase in team size.

Share Content with PR and Marketing Teams

In addition to striving for seamless collaboration and sharing within the advocacy team, advocates should also seek out ways to collaborate with other stakeholders in the business.

One simple and effective way to do this is to work with public relations (PR) and marketing teams to create content. Even though (as Chapter 5 explained) advocacy content is often different from marketing content, there is typically at least some overlap between the content advocates produce and the content that PR and marketing teams leverage. By working with these teams, advocates can reduce the time they spend developing content. Simultaneously, they can increase the reach of their content by placing some of it in the distribution channels maintained by PR and marketing.

As an example of how advocates can collaborate with PR and marketing around content, consider a marketing team that wants to create a banner ad that reaches external developers. Advocates who engage with those developers on a regular basis, and who have a technical background, are likely to be able to generate more effective copy for the ad than marketers could produce on their own. By collaborating with marketing on this initiative, advocates can contribute value to the business. In return, advocates get an opportunity to shape messaging targeted at their external communities of focus, and they don't have to work on their own to produce the content that spreads this messaging.

As another example of opportunities for collaboration, take a PR team that is running an earned media campaign. Earned media is content that mentions a business or its products but is not actually produced by that business. To help generate earned media content, a PR team could place advocates in touch with third-party journalists who can interview and quote them for articles that will appear on external media sites. In this way, advocates get a chance to share their points of view through content, but they don't have to produce or distribute the content on their own. At the same time, the PR team benefits from an easy way to place the company's point of view in front of external audiences.

(Parenthetically, an important challenge to consider is that PR teams, in particular, have a tendency to be very sensitive to advocacies' engagement with news and industry. PR leads may want to exert tight control over what advocates say or which technical opinions they express, because they believe it's important that those opinions align with the company's brand and high-level messaging. There is value in ensuring some level of consistency between what advocates say and what the company believes, but it's important to give advocates latitude and avoid placing artificial limits on their ability to stir up interest and engagement. The company line is not always the best line for reaching external audiences, and PR teams should be willing to grant advocates some leeway to express their opinions, even if the opinions don't perfectly align with top-level messaging.)

A third example of a juncture where advocates can partner with PR and marketing teams is surrounding demand-generation (or demand gen, for short) operations, which focus on generating interest in products or services among prospective customers.

Advocates can help marketers, in particular, with demand gen by sharing some of the content they produce for advocacy purposes to support demand gen operations. In many instances, the types of blog posts, tutorials, and similar content that advocates create to spark engagement with external developers lend themselves well to demand gen, because that content can also help marketers to demonstrate to external developers why they might be interested in a product or tool. For their part, advocates benefit from another distribution channel for content that they have already created, which amplifies their impact without requiring an amplification of effort.

Collaborating on Technical Events

Working with other stakeholders inside the business to help organize and produce content for events is another means of scaling up advocates' impact.

The part of the organization that manages events can vary. The task often falls to marketing teams, but at companies that have a developer relations department, it may handle events that target technical audiences.

Regardless of who within the business is organizing events, advocates can support them through practices such as the following:

- **Curating event topic tracks, speakers, and abstracts:** For technical events, advocates are likely to understand what's topical and what's not better than most other stakeholders, so they can provide unique insight on which content and speakers the business should use to drive the event.

- **Serving as speakers themselves:** Although the business will typically want to send other individuals, and not just as advocates, to speak, advocates are obvious candidates for giving technical talks.

- **Attending events and in-person engagement:** This practice benefits the business as a whole by amplifying its presence at the events. For advocates, it's another way to reach external audiences.

- **Producing lead-up and post-event content**, such as blog posts and emails.

No matter how exactly advocates factor into events, events provide them an opportunity to shine. They can create relationships with external communities and demonstrate credibility for the company. They also enjoy an opportunity to flex their technical muscle and showcase why they are passionate about the company's products. And they make event organizers' work easier in the process.

A final note on events: In some cases, businesses approach events primarily as a way to generate leads (meaning prospective buyers for a company's services or products). This perspective makes sense from the viewpoint of marketing. But for the purposes of advocacy, events should not serve simply as lead-gen opportunities. Aside from the fact that most leads that come out of events are usually not very strong (because event attendees are inundated with messaging from many vendors and may or may not have a strong interest in any one company's offerings), it's important to recognize that events are one of the most authentic and deep opportunities for advocates to engage with external developers. Events are the only place where they can connect face-to-face with their target audiences. As such, events should be places where advocates focus on building relationships, not pushing products or acquiring leads. Leave the marketing to the marketers, even if advocates indirectly support marketing efforts by participating in events.

Conclusion

In a world of limitless budgets and bottomless talent pools, businesses could scale up the impact of developer advocacy operations by simply hiring more advocates. But that's not the world that organizations operate in today. Making the most of advocacy requires unlocking strategies that help advocates work smarter, but not harder, in their engagement with both external and internal stakeholders. They can do this by collaborating closely with each other, as well as reinforcing the efforts of other business units in ways that are mutually beneficial to all parties.

Measuring Advocacy's Impact

Throughout this book, we've touched on the importance of measuring the impact of developer advocates and developer advocacy investments. But we haven't said much about exactly how you do that. We held off because measurement is arguably the most complex facet of developer advocacy operations, and you can't chart an effective measurement strategy until you understand all of the other factors that go into advocacy.

But now that we've discussed those other factors in detail, we're finally ready to talk about measuring the impact of developer advocacy.

Why Measure Impact?

The reasons why you should measure the impact of advocacy are straight-forward enough. For the business, measurement helps leadership teams track how much value advocates are creating. Impact metrics can also help to highlight areas where advocates are proving especially valuable and in which

© Chris Riley, Chris Tozzi 2023
C. Riley and C. Tozzi, *Developer Advocacy*,
https://doi.org/10.1007/978-1-4842-9597-7_9

the business might therefore benefit by investing even more. Likewise, they may reveal aspects of advocacy that are not delivering their intended value so that the business can look deeper into why that is the case and whether advocacy strategies need to shift.

Meanwhile, from the perspectives of advocates themselves, measuring impact is critical for justifying the investment that the business has made in advocacy, demonstrating its value and requesting further growth of advocacy programs. This is especially true given that advocacy's impact is less tangibly self-evident to some business stakeholders than that of many other business units. Most executives understand the intrinsic value of marketing, sales, and engineering departments, for example, but they may be more skeptical of advocacy, given that it is a relatively new type of function. Being able to quantify the impact of advocacy efforts is therefore critical for encouraging buy-in to advocacy initiatives among business leaders.

The Challenge of Measurement

If the importance of measuring advocacy's impact is easy enough to recognize, actually measuring it is much harder.

The main reason why is that traditional business metrics that map directly onto the impact of advocacy programs are in short supply. You can't, for example, attribute revenue in a straightforward way to advocates – and even if you could, you probably shouldn't, because the value of advocacy programs is not simply to increase revenue or drive sales – nor can you (to take another example) measure advocacy's impact by tracking technical metrics like how quickly external support requests are handled or how fast developers build new application features. Here again, although advocates may play some role in these processes, the purpose of advocates is not merely to complement or extend technical departments, and so tracking basic technical operational metrics isn't a good way of measuring the impact of advocates.

On top of this, there is the challenge that if the business settles on a small handful of simple metrics to track, those metrics may end up pushing advocates to operate in ways that don't reflect their true value. If, for example, you measure each advocate's effectiveness simply in terms of how many blog posts they publish per month or how many speaking engagements they record, you end up encouraging advocates to prioritize these activities at the expense of others.

This is a problem that applies to virtually any type of impact measurement, of course, not just advocacy. When you measure any department's or employee's success in terms of simplistic metrics, you end up rewarding some types of behavior and disincentivizing others in ways that may not align with business interests.

However, this problem is especially severe in the case of advocacy, because by its nature, advocacy is a somewhat scrappy type of job whose impact hinges, to a large extent, on the creativity and personal initiative of individual advocates. If you encumber your advocates with simplistic metrics that discourage them from operating in whichever ways yield the greatest impact on their target communities, you are likely to end up with advocates who appear to be underperforming because you measure their impact in the wrong ways – or who appear impactful on paper because they hit the desired numbers, when in actuality, their impact is not as great as it could be because they are forced to game a measurement system that doesn't necessarily reward the most impactful activities.

Yet, despite these substantial challenges, we believe you can measure the impact of advocacy effectively. Doing so may require you to track more metrics, and to quantify data in less traditional ways, than you would when measuring other business functions. You'll also need to tailor your measurement operations to the unique aspects of your advocacy program. But given enough consideration and data collection – and provided the metrics you track and consistent and measurable over time – you can effectively understand the impact and value of individual advocates and of the advocacy team as a whole.

To provide guidance, the rest of this chapter walks through different metrics that you might consider tracking. We break them into two categories:

- Volume metrics, which are relatively simple data points that track the overall activity of advocates
- Impact metrics, more complex metrics tied to how effectively advocates achieve their goals

Most businesses should track a collection of metrics drawn from both categories. We will explain more about the pros and cons of each type of metric and when it makes sense to track it.

Volume Metrics

Volume metrics are more simplistic in nature and less valuable for measuring impact because they track what advocates do and how frequently they do it – data points that are not necessarily reflective of how impactful advocates' work is.

Nonetheless, volume metrics are valuable because they are comparatively easy to collect, and they provide a meaningful, if blunt, means of assessing the overall activity of the advocacy function.

Examples of volume metrics you might track include

- Number of published posts by advocates
- Number of internal tickets advocates have responded to
- Speaking sessions at conferences or industry events

Again, an advocate who performs well based on these metrics will not necessarily be an impactful advocate. An advocate who prolifically authors blog posts, for example, may simply be writing blog posts that few people in their target community read.

Still, by tracking these volume metrics, you can at least chart how busy your advocates appear to be. Plus, you can correlate these metrics with the impact metrics we will discuss to gain more context into which advocate activities drive the most value. If your advocates are increasing their in-person event attendance but in-person events are not driving engagement, for example, it's a sign that advocates should invest more time in other initiatives.

Impact Metrics

In general, impact metrics are more difficult to track because it's not always possible to collect the data in a way that is pegged directly to impact. For example, if you want to know how impactful a blog post was, you could track how data like many people viewed the article and how long they spent on the page reading it. However, those metrics alone don't align perfectly with impact, because they don't allow you to measure how many people were meaningfully influenced by the blog, or how much engagement it drove with developer audiences.

Yet, despite the imperfect nature of impact metrics, they're the best data source available to you for understanding how much overall engagement your advocates are achieving.

Here's a look at impact metrics worth tracking.

Share of Conversation

Share of conversation is a metric that assesses the impact of content based on the number of times that mentions of your products, services, or APIs appear in organic content, such as third-party blog posts or social media conversations. Tracking share of conversation is complex because it requires the ability to pull data from multiple sources – some of which you may not even know about – and this is therefore a challenging metric to work with. However, it's one of the most valuable for measuring overall impact because the more often practitioners are talking about the technical solutions that advocates promote, the more effective the advocates are sharing insights and driving interest in those solutions.

Importantly, share of conversation is distinct from share of voice, a metric commonly used by public relations organizations. To calculate share of voice, businesses simply count the number of times that content is shared. But because content sharing often happens automatically, this is an easy metric to game, and it doesn't closely align with impact.

Share of conversation goes deeper. It allows you to answer questions like "How many times did developers on Stack Overflow mention our API as a way to solve a technical challenge?" and "How many tutorials about our product did third-party developers voluntarily write on Medium just to show off how the product works?" Instead of tracking the relatively meaningless metric of article shares, you measure the frequency with which your brand, product, feature, or API shows up in relevant technical conversations.

Time to Solution

Time to solution measures the average time it takes a developer to build a solution based on a company's product or services. It's hard to measure, but you can ascertain it by tracking when a development project began and when it had its first production instance.

The value of the time to solution metric is that it reflects – albeit in a somewhat crude, complex way – how easily external developers are able to leverage the solutions that advocates share with them. If it takes external developers a long time to build solutions based on your APIs, for example, it's a sign that either your APIs are too complex (in which case your product team may need to find ways to simplify them) or that external audiences simply don't understand how to use them, partly because advocates are not doing their jobs as well as they could.

Activations and Signups

As we explain in the following, attempting to track how many leads advocates generate is not very useful. But it can be valuable to track signups, product activations, or other types of engagement that can be attributed to content produced by advocates.

This is because these activities are a reflection of meaningful community engagement. Not everyone who activates a product is necessarily a qualified lead, but most people who start testing a product because of a blog post by an advocate are engaged audience members.

API Endpoint Metrics

The more external developers are using your company's products, the higher the activity you should see on API endpoints. Thus, by tracking this technical data, you can get a sense of how product engagement changes over time.

The major caveat is that not all API endpoint trends can be attributed to external engagement. They are also affected by factors like the volume at which existing customers use a product or service and how widely third-party integrations are deployed (which is different from how many third-party integrations are built). Still, as a means of gaining context on overall engagement trends, API endpoint metrics have value.

Audience Growth

Since one of the chief goals of advocates is to increase the number of developers who are engaged with a company's ecosystem, tracking the total size of external developer audiences is a valuable means of assessing advocacy's total impact.

Measuring audience growth is tricky in the respect that the audiences in question typically operate across diverse media and have varying levels of engagement. Still, you can gain consistent insight into the general size of developer audiences by tracking the total number of subscribers on digital platforms and channels, such as blogs that your company owns, product demo websites, and third-party media sites (like YouTube) where your advocates post content. You can also track total attendees at technical events that your business sponsors, or how many people visit booths or attend speaking sessions focused on your products or services.

When measuring audiences and audience growth, be sure to differentiate subscribers from generic visitors. In general, to count as an audience member, a user should have recurring engagement with a channel or platform and should be automatically notified when new content is released. This is what differentiates your audience from your total user visitor base.

Blog Traffic

The preceding point notwithstanding, there is also value in measuring the overall traffic to blogs and other digital platforms that your advocates manage or where they post content. Although not everyone who is a visitor can be considered an audience member, traffic volume is a measure of how much overall impact your digital content has on external communities.

This is a crude impact metric that only tells part of the story. But it's also easy to collect, since in most cases you can track traffic without significant effort.

Per-Content Traffic

In addition to tracking traffic to blogs or digital platforms as a whole, you can track how many people read or engage with specific pieces of content – such as a particular article on a blog.

This type of measurement is useful in general for understanding which types of content or topics are most engaging, and it's worth collecting in order to give advocates a stronger sense of what their audiences want most.

That said, we don't recommend per-content traffic measurement as a primary means of assessing the impact of advocacy as a whole. The reason why is that the total page views that an individual content item receives may vary depending on a variety of factors – such as the time of day when it originally appeared and whether users repost or share it on external sites – that are beyond the control of the advocate who produced the content. Some content ends up "going viral" in ways that are hard to explain, other than attributing their success to luck. In other cases, strong content that has great potential ends up buried and receiving little engagement.

Coupled with the fact that, as we noted previously, metrics like total page views aren't necessarily a reflection of the actual engagement or impact of content, these factors mean that it's unwise to read too much into the success of individual content items. It's better to focus on trends that span across all content.

Social Engagement

Social media platforms offer various types of data points that, to a limited extent, offer limited opportunity for measuring engagement. You can track how many external users follow an advocate on Twitter, for instance, or how often their posts are "liked" on LinkedIn.

Here again, however, we strongly caution against giving metrics like these too much weight, because various factors beyond the advocate's control can affect social engagement metrics. For example, the way that a social media platform's algorithm promotes (or doesn't promote) a post could have a tremendous impact on the engagement it receives.

On top of this, there is the problem that engagement on social media platforms rarely maps cleanly onto real-world engagement or impact. An advocate who has a large number of Twitter followers may just be good at acquiring Twitter followers, not at engaging with developers in impactful ways.

Reduction in Support Requests

Since part of the job of advocates is to help external developers understand how to use product features effectively, good advocacy should result in fewer technical support requests.

That said, if you track this metric, be careful not to end up putting advocates in a position where providing user support becomes their primary mission. Advocates should produce content and best practices that help external users to leverage products effectively, but they should not be troubleshooting developer problems all day long.

Metrics *Not* to Track

You may notice that certain metrics that appear frequently in measurements of business impact are missing from our list of advocacy metrics. We'd like to mention them briefly so it's clear why we don't think you should track this data as a way of measuring advocacy's impact.

- **Leads:** As we said earlier in the book, advocates may help to support marketing and sales staff and even collaborate with them around content and engagement. But advocates are not marketers or salespeople, and their purpose is not merely to generate leads.

- **Revenue:** Along similar lines, advocates' jobs are not directly linked to revenue generation. Plus, it's virtually impossible to attribute revenue to advocates, even if you really wanted to. (That said, we'll say more about revenue tracking and its link to advocacy in the following.)

- **Live event attendance:** We don't recommend tracking how many people attend live events where advocates speak in person or online. The reason why is that attendance at individual events can be affected by many factors (like the location of an in-person event or the time of day of an online webinar) that are beyond advocates' control.

- **Product trials or downloads:** How often external developers download a product or sign up for a trial may not directly measure advocates' work product. Developers won't necessarily do anything with a download or trial. It's better to focus on tracking how developers use products and trials, not how often they sign up for them.

The bottom line here is that it's important not to group advocates in with other business functions when measuring impact. Advocacy is a unique function that must be assessed in unique ways.

Metrics Correlation: A Note on Revenue Measurement and Advocacy

We've made clear earlier that we don't think advocates should be measured (or should measure themselves) based on how much revenue they generate. Beyond the fact that it's very difficult to attribute any revenue directly to advocates given that they are not in a sales role, focusing on revenue-related metrics can cause businesses to mistake advocates for marketers, which they are not.

That said, the reality is that sooner or later, every business function is measured at least partly on revenue. Advocacy teams – and their supporters within the business – can therefore benefit by getting ahead of the narrative surrounding revenue and present data that highlights how they contribute to revenue generation.

Doing so is easy enough, given that advocacy touches on all stages of the sales and marketing funnel, even though it doesn't own any of them. Specifically, advocacy can be linked to revenue based on metrics like the following:

- **New active developers:** The more developers who sign up for a product and actually use it, the higher the revenue impact of advocates likely is.

- **Revenue touched:** A measure of how much revenue is indirectly attributable to advocate activities. This is a powerful metric when calculated correctly over an extended period of time. The best way to calculate this is to track engagement with developer content (such as content views) and store that activity as a record for a contact in your CRM. Then, you can decide if you want to calculate how many contacts who view advocacy content are part of a sales opportunity, or calculate total monthly revenue based on the content from the advocates.

- **Revenue protected:** Advocates can help to protect revenue by playing a role in retaining existing customers. This work can be measured in a manner similar to revenue touched: Look at the number of customers up for renewal who ended up renewing, and correlate that data with the number of customers who engaged with advocacy content or with advocates themselves.

Thus, there are effective ways of quantifying how advocates influence revenue, even though revenue-centric measurements should never be at the core of strategies for assessing advocacy's impact.

Conclusion

Advocacy can't function effectively or efficiently over the long term unless its value can be quantified, nor can advocates identify new opportunities or understand where they are making the greatest impact in the absence of systematic measurement of their activity.

While measuring advocate impact is not as straightforward as measuring impact for other types of functions, it's possible. Advocates, in collaboration with other stakeholders in the business, must decide on which metrics to track and how to leverage that data both to prove the value of advocacy and to help advocates operate as effectively as possible.

Parting Thoughts on Successful Developer Advocacy

If you've read this far into the book, you should have a pretty good sense of what developer advocacy means, what advocates do, and how they bring value to the business. You should also know more than a little about how to establish an advocacy function within an organization, how to grow it, how to maximize its impact, and how to track the effectiveness of advocacy operations over time. In other words, you've learned the fundamentals of developer advocacy from the perspectives of both advocates themselves and the businesses they support.

© Chris Riley, Chris Tozzi 2023
C. Riley and C. Tozzi, *Developer Advocacy*,
https://doi.org/10.1007/978-1-4842-9597-7_10

In this final chapter, we want to address some topics that don't map cleanly onto the other subjects we've discussed in this book. Specifically, we'll explain what *not* to do in the realm of developer advocacy. Then, we'll talk about where to go next once you've established a successful, scalable, measurable, and self-sustaining advocacy program.

We saved this content for the last chapter because it doesn't apply to all businesses or advocates. You may or may not run into the pitfalls we'll cover in the "what not to do" part of this, and you may or may not grow your advocacy program to the point where you can explore the suggestions about where to go next after you've excelled in all other areas of advocacy. But some organizations will benefit from this advice – and even if yours doesn't, we hope this chapter offers useful context that helps you think more broadly and strategically about developer advocacy, regardless of whether the guidance applies specifically to you.

Common Developer Advocacy Mistakes

Let's start with mistakes organizations sometimes make when building or scaling developer advocacy programs. We've touched on some of these mistakes in earlier chapters, but we didn't elaborate on them in detail.

Mistake #1: Unrealistic Expectations

Perhaps the easiest mistake to make when implementing a developer advocacy function within a business is having unrealistic expectations about how impactful the program will be and/or about how quickly it will yield a measurable impact.

You might launch an advocacy program and expect that within just a few months, you'll begin seeing a significant uptick in engagement among external developers with your business. This mindset is especially common among startups, which are accustomed to expecting rapid change across many facets of the business. It's also informed by the fact that in unusual cases (companies like Docker and Twilio come to mind), massive external developer engagement does occur on a rapid timeline.

But those companies' stories are the exception, not the norm. It's important to have realistic expectations about how long it will take for developer advocacy to begin moving the needle. Exactly how long that period might be depends on various factors, such as how many resources your business invests in advocacy, how mature its software platform and tools are, and which types of developers it's seeking to engage with. But in general, expect a period of many months, if not a year or longer, before you begin noticing a real impact from your advocacy program.

Having realistic expectations in this regard is important, of course, because without them, businesses might conclude prematurely that investing in advocacy was a mistake and pull the plug on the initiative. Instead, they should give advocacy the time it needs to make an impact on how external developers perceive the businesses' brands and products.

Mistake #2: Treating Advocates As Celebrities

Another common mistake – and one that we see most often made by smaller companies looking to make as big a splash as possible within external developer communities – is to assume that advocates should operate like, and ideally be, celebrities within developer communities.

When businesses adopt this mindset, they focus on hiring advocates who have large followings within technical communities. They hope that these people will yield the greatest engagement on the shortest timeline, since they're already known to their target audiences.

This approach is a mistake for several reasons. One is that the pool of prospective advocates who count as celebrities within technical communities is very small, so hiring them is a real challenge. Another is that people with large followings don't always have the broad set of skills necessary to succeed as advocates. Just because a certain developer has a lot of Twitter followers doesn't mean they are also adept at performing internal advocacy work, for example, or at generating the long-form technical content that is an important component of advocate output.

On top of this, there is the risk that someone with a large preexisting following will be seen as "selling out" if they join a company and begin promoting its products to technical users. As we've said, developers tend to be allergic to anything that looks or feels like inauthentic marketing efforts.

So, instead of centering your business's advocacy strategy around finding and hiring the handfuls of people who are already famous within technical communities, look for individuals who can check off the unique set of skills that advocacy requires – like technical chops, the ability to understand multiple aspects of the business, and a knack for creating and sharing content – even if they lack celebrity status.

Just as important, don't assume that your advocates are failures if they don't gain celebrity status over time. As long as they're making an impact, they're a success; few advocates gain anything resembling real fame.

Mistake #3: Hiring Advocacy Managers Before Advocates

Given the novelty of the developer advocacy function to most businesses, it can be tempting for organizations to decide that they should hire a developer advocacy manager or director in order to launch the function. That person, they might think, can do the hard work of figuring out what advocates need to do and then finding and hiring individual advocates.

We think this top-down approach to building out the advocacy function is a mistake because people with the skills and willingness to run an advocacy function are often not primed to carry out day-to-day advocacy work, like creating and sharing content. As a result, trying to hire managers or directors before actual advocates significantly delays the time it takes to get up and running with advocacy and start making an impact. There is also the problem that a top-heavy advocacy program will be expensive, and there is a risk that managers hired into these roles won't actually know much about advocacy, given the uniqueness of the discipline.

So, a healthier, safer, and more cost-effective approach to launching an advocacy program is to start with advocates themselves. Even if they lack advocacy managers or directors to report to initially, they can begin doing advocacy work under the direction of other leaders within the business – such as marketing teams – until the advocacy function can be built out and a dedicated management structure can be implemented.

Mistake #4: Hiring Advocacy-Focused Managers

On the other hand, it's also a mistake to build out an advocacy program in a bottom-up fashion and assume that you can create a management team for advocates by drawing solely from the advocates themselves. In other words, you hire advocates and then expect some of them to run the program as managers.

The problem with this approach is that there is limited overlap between the skills necessary to be a good advocate and the skills necessary to manage advocates. Although there are certainly instances where someone with an advocacy background can also excel in leading an advocacy team, we recommend that, in general, businesses build out their advocacy management teams by focusing on individuals who are solid leaders, regardless of whether they come from an advocacy background.

Mistake #5: Not Making Advocacy Its Own Function

No matter how you go about building out your advocacy team, you may struggle to determine exactly where advocacy should fit within your business. The multifaceted nature of advocacy programs means that it's hard to classify advocacy; it's part software development, part marketing, part sales (at least indirectly), and part product management.

The wrong way to fit advocacy into the business is to force it to operate under the guise of one of these other functions. We've seen some organizations do this because they really want advocacy to fit neatly within existing organizational structures, and since there is overlap between advocacy and various other functions, they think it's reasonable enough to insert advocacy into one of those functions.

That doesn't work well, though, for the obvious reason that advocacy spans many different traditional business functions. If you try to operate advocacy under the umbrella of just one function, you risk misclassifying it or depriving it of its full impact.

Instead, the best way to run an advocacy program is to make it a dedicated function. As we noted earlier in the book, this isn't always possible when your advocacy program is just starting out, but as you scale up, you should be treating advocacy as a unique, stand-alone function, not a component or extension of other parts of the business.

Be Boring

Now that you know what not to do as you establish and grow an advocacy program, let's pivot toward discussing where to go once you have an advocacy function up and running at scale within your business.

We can sum up our guidance on this front with two words: be boring. At its best, advocacy when fully grown should be a boring function of your business. Just like sales, marketing, and product development, a mature advocacy program should be status quo, delivering value on a regular and predictable basis.

We're not saying you should avoid any kind of experimentation. On the contrary, your advocates should always be looking for novel ways to engage developer audiences, such as by creating first-of-its-kind content. And you should expect to have to adjust your advocacy team over time as advocates come and go and as the developer audiences and/or products you are promoting to them change.

But on the whole, you should avoid earth-shattering changes to your advocacy function once it is established. Don't implement radical changes, such as trying to restructure the program or adopting fundamentally new strategies.

This is an important point because a "boring" advocacy program is one that has clear direction and stability. Boringness ensures that the value of your program for the business won't come under constant scrutiny and that your advocates won't be redirected toward projects (like writing documentation) that they are not well-suited to support.

In turn, a boring advocacy function is one where advocates themselves can thrive. They're free from interruptions and distractions, and they can focus on doing more of what they're good at: engaging with internal and external audiences around technical products in creative ways.

Conclusion

If you asked us to tie this chapter – or even this entire book – into just a few paragraphs of parting advice, we'd tell you that the key to successful advocacy is to think realistically and stay grounded. No matter where you are on your developer advocacy journey – whether you're just evaluating how advocacy could benefit your business, you have started an advocacy function that you're now scaling, or you have a full-fledged advocacy program in operation – the key to effectiveness is to have a realistic understanding of what advocacy can do and pursue it in a practical way.

We emphasize this because having worked in the technology industry for years, we know that unrealistic expectations and rash thinking are all too common. Everyone wants a unicorn, and they want it right away. To be sure, this type of thinking rewards some companies. Being boring or settling for predictability instead of taking chances on radical initiatives isn't always enough to stand out in the highly competitive world of tech.

But running an advocacy program isn't the same as founding a software company or inventing a new product. It shouldn't be disruptive; it should be a way to bring steady value to your business by helping internal and external stakeholders understand your technical products. When you approach advocacy from this grounded, steady-minded perspective, you're primed for success.

I

Index